Book Two

ESL Reading & Writing, Etc.

A Basic English Literacy Program

Judith S. Rubenstein   •   Janet M. Gubbay

National Textbook Company
NTC a division of NTC Publishing Group • Lincolnwood, Illinois USA

To our husbands,
Howard S. Rubenstein and
Jacob D. Gubbay,
whose encouragement and support
made this possible

Published by National Textbook Company, a division of NTC Publishing
Group.
© 1989 by NTC Publishing Group, 4255 West Touhy Avenue,
Lincolnwood (Chicago), Illinois 60646-1975 U.S.A.
Manufactured in the United States of America.
9 0 ML 9 8 7 6 5 4 3 2 1

Contents

Preface

Essentials of Reading and Writing English is a three-book series that offers students the opportunity to develop basic reading and writing skills in English. In addition, the material in these books will help students to improve their pronunciation as they become familiar with the sounds of English and the ways in which these sounds correspond to the written language. The three books in this series may be used independently or as a set by students of English as a first or second language who want to acquire basic reading and writing skills in English.

Essentials of Reading and Writing English teaches students to read English using a phonetic approach because English is a phonetic language: All the words in the English language are formed from a combination of the twenty-six letters of the alphabet, and the sounds of these letters are limited and predictable. All the lessons in the series are presented using a format similar to the formats used in newspapers, magazines, mail, and books. The lines and spaces provided for students to write in are a standard size, like those found on typical forms at a bank, doctor's office, school, employment agency, or government office. The reading passages in the book reflect adult responsibilities and real-life situations within the limits of the lesson vocabulary.

Book Two of the series emphasizes multisyllabic short-vowel words, blends, and related sight words in word lists, sentences, and stories. While the levels are progressively challenging, the student is prepared for each new level by the preceding work. Using the skills learned in Book One or comparable materials, the student is empowered to read long words by attaching one short-vowel syllable to the next.

With multisyllabic words and blends, the content of the stories in Book Two vastly expands to cover topics of various workplaces, health, law, interpersonal relations, and recreation. The style of the stories goes beyond the standard paragraph to include newspaper formats, work lists, and quotations. The phonetic content of each story emphasizes the current lesson and includes skills taught in previous chapters.

Special sounds are introduced in Book Two, but all are presented within the predictable context of the five short vowels, their related exceptions, and material already learned. Every new sound is taught individually and systematically on a "Sound" page, and there is space to "Read," "Write," and "Listen and write" the sound, related words, and sentences. These activities both reinforce and measure learning. Also included in this book are common idioms, names, and geographical terms, all of which are relevant to success in the world. The student can now recognize and read them using the multisyllabic, short-vowel skills taught in Book Two.

Book One presents the alphabet in print, script, and book type, plus one-syllable, three-letter, short-vowel words. Book Three covers long-vowel words and sentences, special sounds, and related sight words.

Essentials of Reading and Writing English, with its clear format and easy-to-follow approach, simplifies the task of learning to read, write, and pronounce English. We have grouped words into meaningful patterns and provided a means of building essential reading and writing skills in English by presenting material in small, easily mastered increments. At the same time, the series offers mastery of a very complex curriculum.

Through using the three books in the *Essentials of Reading and Writing English* series, students will experience increased self-confidence and find success and pleasure in learning to read and write English.

Judith S. Rubenstein and Janet M. Gubbay

Acknowledgments

I want to express my gratitude to those persons and teachers in the field of education who have had the greatest influence on me: Dr. John B. Carroll, Roy Edward Larsen Professor of Educational Psychology, Emeritus, and former Director of the Laboratory for Research in Instruction, Harvard Graduate School of Education, and Dr. Fletcher G. Watson, Henry Lee Shattuck Professor of Education, Emeritus, Harvard Graduate School of Education, both of whom inspired and guided my graduate work; Eloise Gredler who, in her home-school, demonstrated to me the power of phonics for teaching reading; my students, who stimulated me to create materials that could help them, and on whom I tested the lessons in these books; Rebecca Rauff, ESL/EFL Editor, National Textbook Company, who so carefully and skillfully edited the manuscript; Kathleen Schultz, ESL/EFL Editor, National Textbook Company, who provided valuable assistance in the final stages of the project; and finally to Janet M. Gubbay, my co-author, who first suggested we undertake to write this series together and who has been a tireless, creative, and ideal partner since the beginning.

These volumes could not have been realized, however, without the support of my family. I am especially grateful to my husband, Howard S. Rubenstein, for his enthusiasm for this project from the start and for many helpful suggestions; to my children, Emily, Adam, Jennifer, and John, for their overall sense of humor and cooperation and spontaneous contributions of ideas; and to both my mother, Martha K. Selig, and my father, the late Dr. Kalman Selig, whose love of books and learning has been my ultimate teacher.

Judith S. Rubenstein

CHAPTER 1:
Two-Syllable, Short-Vowel Words and Names

In this chapter, you will review vowels, consonants, and one-syllable, short-vowel words.

You will also read, write, and review

► two-syllable, short-vowel words and names

► the sight words **for, or, want, too,** and **women**

► three-syllable, short-vowel words as a bonus

► sentences and a story that emphasize these lessons

Introduction to Two-Syllable, Short-Vowel Words

A. REVIEW OF VOWELS AND CONSONANTS

There are five vowels in the English language.   They are **a, e, i, o, u** (and sometimes **y**).

You already have learned the short sound for each vowel:

ă as in **a**pple

ĕ as in **e**gg

ĭ as in **i**nch

ŏ as in **o**live

ŭ as in **u**mbrella

All the other letters of the alphabet are called consonants:

b, c, d, f, g, h, j, k, l, m, n, p, q, r, s, t, v, w, x, z (and sometimes y)

1. Circle the vowels:

a b c d e f g h i j k l m n o p q r s t u v w x y z

2. Circle the consonants:

a b c d e f g h i j k l m n o p q r s t u v w x y z

B. REVIEW OF ONE-SYLLABLE WORDS

A one-syllable word has one vowel sound.   For example:

> ca**t** has the one vowel sound ă
>
> p**i**t has the one vowel sound ĭ

Read and circle the short vowels in these words:

> get hop sum pan mix Mel Jill

C. TWO-SYLLABLE, SHORT-VOWEL WORDS

In this book, you will learn to read short-vowel words and names with two syllables, such as **sunset**.

Two-syllable words are words that have two separate vowel sounds.   For example, in the two-syllable word **sunset**, the first vowel sound is the ŭ in **sun**. The second vowel sound is the ĕ in **set**:

s**u**n s**e**t

1. Say each vowel sound: ŭ ĕ

2. Say each syllable slowly: **sun set**

3. Clap your hands each time you say a syllable: **sun set**
    Then say the syllables again: **sun set**

4. Now say the two syllables closer together: **sun set**

5. Now say the two-syllable word: **sunset**

6. Write the two-syllable word:

> sunset _____
>
> sunset _____
>
> sunset _____

100 Two-Syllable, Short-Vowel Words*

Say each syllable slowly.   Then say the syllables close together.   Read and write the two-syllable words.

Read syllables:	Read words:	Write:	
1. sun set	sunset	sunset	*sunset*
2. hub cap	hubcap		
3. rab bit	rabbit		
4. nap kin	napkin		
5. cab in	cabin		
6. cam el	camel		
7. ban dit	bandit		
8. kit ten	kitten		
9. ton ic	tonic		
10. ten nis	tennis		
11. com ic	comic		
12. sal ad	salad		
13. bas ket	basket		
14. hab it	habit		
15. nut meg	nutmeg		
16. sud den	sudden		
17. muf fin	muffin		
18. den im	denim		
19. at tic	attic		
20. tal ent	talent		
21. cac tus	cactus		
22. vis it	visit		
23. com mit	commit		
24. sev en	seven		

*See Appendix B for an alphabetized list of all the words presented through page 12.

Read syllables:	Read words:	Write:	
25. an tic	antic	_____	_____
26. up set	upset	_____	_____
27. cof fin	coffin	_____	_____
28. pub lic	public	_____	_____
29. less en	lessen	_____	_____
30. com bat	combat	_____	_____
31. com et	comet	_____	_____
32. hap pen	happen	_____	_____
33. can not	cannot	_____	_____
34. got ten	gotten	_____	_____
35. pic nic	picnic	_____	_____
36. cat nip	catnip	_____	_____
37. hid den	hidden	_____	_____
38. up on	upon	_____	_____
39. rap id	rapid	_____	_____
40. caf tan	caftan	_____	_____
41. ex am	exam	_____	_____
42. tab let	tablet	_____	_____
43. mit ten	mitten	_____	_____
44. car rot	carrot	_____	_____
45. lim it	limit	_____	_____
46. con fess	confess	_____	_____
47. can did	candid	_____	_____
48. vom it	vomit	_____	_____
49. ton sils	tonsils	_____	_____

Read syllables:	Read words:	Write:	
50. a go	ago	_____	_____
51. ful fill	fulfill	_____	_____
52. cam pus	campus	_____	_____
53. sol id	solid	_____	_____
54. sub mit	submit	_____	_____
55. can vas	canvas	_____	_____
56. tid bit	tidbit	_____	_____
57. rot ten	rotten	_____	_____
58. a miss	amiss	_____	_____
59. sub let	sublet	_____	_____
60. vic tim	victim	_____	_____
61. mag net	magnet	_____	_____
62. liq uid	liquid	_____	_____
63. tac tic	tactic	_____	_____
64. em bed	embed	_____	_____
65. hec tic	hectic	_____	_____
66. hel met	helmet	_____	_____
67. a mid	amid	_____	_____
68. Kan sas	Kansas	_____	_____
69. len tils	lentils	_____	_____
70. pel vis	pelvis	_____	_____
71. sat in	satin	_____	_____
72. lin en	linen	_____	_____
73. mus lin	muslin	_____	_____
74. quin tet	quintet	_____	_____
75. pup pet	puppet	_____	_____
76. ad mit	admit	_____	_____
77. cut let	cutlet	_____	_____

Read syllables:	Read words:	Write:	
78. pal lid	pallid	_____	_____
79. kid nap	kidnap	_____	_____
80. com pass	compass	_____	_____
81. gav el	gavel	_____	_____
82. mal let	mallet	_____	_____
83. rus tic	rustic	_____	_____
84. com pel	compel	_____	_____
85. sun up	sunup	_____	_____
86. cat nap	catnap	_____	_____
87. op tic	optic	_____	_____
88. an nex	annex	_____	_____
89. fat ten	fatten	_____	_____
90. up hill	uphill	_____	_____
91. on set	onset	_____	_____
92. pan el	panel	_____	_____
93. ram rod	ramrod	_____	_____
94. off set	offset	_____	_____
95. zig zag	zigzag	_____	_____
96. val id	valid	_____	_____
97. pan ic	panic	_____	_____
98. wom en	women*	_____	_____
99. bul let	bullet*	_____	_____
100. wel come	welcome*	_____	_____

---

*These are sight words: **women** sounds like **wimmin (wim min)**; in **bullet, bull** sounds like **pull**; in **welcome, come** is a sight word.

Listen and write:

1. _____   26. _____   51. _____

2. _____   27. _____   52. _____

3. _____   28. _____   53. _____

4. _____   29. _____   54. _____

5. _____   30. _____   55. _____

6. _____   31. _____   56. _____

7. _____   32. _____   57. _____

8. _____   33. _____   58. _____

9. _____   34. _____   59. _____

10. _____   35. _____   60. _____

11. _____   36. _____   61. _____

12. _____   37. _____   62. _____

13. _____   38. _____   63. _____

14. _____   39. _____   64. _____

15. _____   40. _____   65. _____

16. _____   41. _____   66. _____

17. _____   42. _____   67. _____

18. _____   43. _____   68. _____

19. _____   44. _____   69. _____

20. _____   45. _____   70. _____

21. _____   46. _____   71. _____

22. _____   47. _____   72. _____

23. _____   48. _____   73. _____

24. _____   49. _____   74. _____

25. _____   50. _____   75. _____

Two-Syllable, Short-Vowel Words Formed with Prefixes and Suffixes

A. PREFIXES: un, ex, mis, dis, im, in

Prefixes come *before* the root word. For example: **un** + fit = unfit

Read:		Write:	Listen and write:
1. **un** fit	unfit	unfit	unfit
2. **un** til	until		
3. **un** cut	uncut		
4. **un** less	unless		
5. **ex** it	exit		
6. **ex** pel	expel		
7. **mis** fit	misfit		
8. **mis** hap	mishap		
9. **mis** led	misled		
10. **dis** cuss	discuss		
11. **dis** miss	dismiss		
12. **dis** pel	dispel		
13. **im** pel	impel		
14. **in** dex	index		
15. **in** put	input		
16. **in** to	into		
17. **in** set	inset		
18. **in** let	inlet		

B. SUFFIXES: ful, less, ness, es (plural)

Suffixes come *after* the root word. For example: will + **ful** = willful

Read:		Write:	Listen and write:
1. will **ful**	willful	*willful* _____	_____
2. fit **ful**	fitful	_____	_____
3. hat **less**	hatless	_____	_____
4. gas **less**	gasless	_____	_____
5. rim **less**	rimless	_____	_____
6. job **less**	jobless	_____	_____
7. fun **less**	funless	_____	_____
8. ill **ness**	illness	_____	_____
9. fit **ness**	fitness	_____	_____
10. sad **ness**	sadness	_____	_____
11. wit **ness**	witness	_____	_____
12. box **es**	boxes	_____	_____
13. mix **es**	mixes	_____	_____
14. mess **es**	messes	_____	_____
15. pass **es**	passes	_____	_____
16. buzz **es**	buzzes	_____	_____

Two-Syllable, Short-Vowel Words and Names in Which **o** Sounds Like **ŭ** (**sun**)

Words and names with the endings **om, on, ton,** and **son**:

Read:		Write:	Listen and write:
om	1. rans**om**		
	2. bott**om**		
	3. cust**om**		
	4. wisd**om**		
	5. seld**om**		
on	6. lem**on**		
	7. wag**on**		
	8. mel**on**		
	9. less**on**		
	10. cany**on**		
	11. fel**on**		
	12. gall**on**		
	13. Lond**on**		
	14. ribb**on**		
ton	15. cott**on**		
	16. butt**on**		
	17. Bos**ton**		
	18. Pax**ton**		
	19. Mil**ton**		
son	20. Wil**son**		
	21. Ben**son**		
	22. Nel**son**		

Two-Syllable, Short-Vowel Names

Say and write the two-syllable names.

WOMEN'S NAMES

Read syllables:	Read name:	Write:	Listen and write:
1. An na	Anna*	Anna	
2. Don na	Donna		
3. Han na	Hanna		
4. Jan et	Janet		
5. Kar en	Karen		
6. El len	Ellen		
7. Lin da	Linda		
8. Meg an	Megan		
9. Rob in	Robin**		
10. Hel en	Helen		

MEN'S NAMES

Read syllables:	Read name:	Write:	Listen and write:
1. Ad am	Adam	Adam	
2. Al len	Allen		
3. An ton	Anton		
4. Cal vin	Calvin		
5. Den nis	Dennis		
6. Ed win	Edwin		
7. Kev in	Kevin		
8. Mel vin	Melvin		
9. Col lin	Collin		
10. Max well	Maxwell		

*a at the end of a word usually sounds like ŭ (rhymes with the)

**Robin is also a man's name.

Sight Words: **for, or, want, too**

1. Read **for**:   Write **for**:

   for For for For for for   *for* _____

   Read: That pen is his, but this pen is **for** you.

   Write: _____

2. Read **or**:   Write **or**:

   or Or or Or or or   _____

   Read: That pen is for you **or** me.

   Write: _____

3. Read **want**:   Write **want**:

   want Want want Want want   _____

   Read: I have a pad, but I **want** a pen.

   Write: _____

4. Read **too**:   Write **too**:

   too Too too Too too too   _____

   Read: She has a pen, so give me a pen, **too.**

   Write: _____

5. Read **for, or, want, too**:   Write **for, or, want, too**:

   for or want too For Or Want Too   _____

   Read: I **want** pads **or** pens **for** her, **too.**

   Write: _____

Listen and write:

1. _____

2. _____

3. _____

4. _____

5. _____

Sentences with Two-Syllable, Short-Vowel Words

Read:

1. Can Allen have a pen for the exam?
2. Melvin and Donna put nutmeg on the salad for the picnic.
3. Have Linda get a gallon of tonic for us, too.
4. Has Megan had seven tennis lessons? She has talent!
5. Anton put carrots, lemons, and melons into his wagon.
6. In the basket are seven hot muffins and a linen napkin.
7. Did he want Dennis to visit him at the cabin?
8. In the comics, Batman and Robin want to get the bandits.
9. A rabbit and a kitten are not as big as a camel.
10. The upset kid has bad tonsils and cannot go to Kansas.
11. Is denim solid blue cotton or muslin?

Write:

1. *Can Allen have a pen for the exam?*

2. _____

3. _____

4. _____

5. _____

6. _____

7. _____

8. _____

9. _____

10. _____

11. _____

Listen and write:

1. _____

2. _____

3. _____

4. _____

5. _____

6. _____

7. _____

8. _____

9. _____

10. _____

11. _____

Story 1

Read: **The Picnic at Cactus Canyon**

The picnic is at Cactus Canyon. It is for the public. It is at 12 noon.   1

Megan and Calvin have some kids, Ellen and Milton. They are at the picnic.   2
Janet and Dennis have some kids, too. They are Edwin and Linda. They have a pen
pal, Anton, with them. They are at the picnic, too. Calvin, Megan, and the kids got to
the picnic in a wagon. Dennis, Janet, and the kids got to it in a bus. They met at
Cactus Canyon. Lots of men, women, and kids are at the picnic.

The dads, moms, and kids sit in the sun. They have big denim hats on. Janet   3
and Dennis have a picnic basket. In the basket, they have hot muffins in a linen
napkin, lots of salad with lentils and lemon, some carrots and a dip with dill, and a
big, uncut melon. Dennis has a gallon of tonic, too, and cups and mugs in a canvas
bag. Megan and Calvin have cutlets and hot dogs on buns. Janet and Megan put
nutmeg on the salad, and Dennis and Calvin put lemon on the melon. Megan and
Calvin have some salad and carrots with the dill dip. The kids want hot dogs and
tonic. They want some carrots and melon, too.

Two rabbits hop up to the kids. The kids give bits of cut carrots to them.   4
Seven robins get a muffin. "Go, you bandits!" said Calvin. "This is not for you!"
Ants and bugs get tidbits of the muffin. Ellen and Megan yell as the bugs nip the legs
of the kids.

Milton and Ellen have pets with them. They have a black and white cat and **5** its seven kittens. The pets run to the kids to get catnip. Edwin and Linda have two dogs at the picnic, too. Will the two dogs nip the cat and its seven kittens? No, that will not happen. The dogs are pals with the kittens and the cat. The dogs run with the cats and do not upset them.

Megan said, "Calvin and I want to jog for fitness. Dennis, will you and Janet **6** come with us?"

Dennis said, "Yes, we will jog, too. We will go for it! But I confess, I have a **7** limit. I cannot run to the summit of the hill. I am too fat!"

"He has talent at tennis and will get fit with his lessons," said Janet. **8**

"You have comic talent, Janet!" said Dennis. **9**

Janet then said to the five kids, "We have lots that we can do for fun until we **10** go. We can hop in a big cotton bag. If you get to the bottom of the hill, you win! We can pull and tug on this ribbon. If you pull the kids to you, and they submit, then you win the combat. We can toss buttons into a basket, too. If you can come up with a compass, we can go to the rim of the canyon, or we can have a catnap!"

It is sunset, and they have to go. The women, men, kids, and pets had lots of **11** fun at the picnic. They had no mishaps and no sadness. The antics of the kids and the pets had not gotten the moms and dads upset. They want to picnic a lot. They want it to be a habit. It is fun to visit with pals at a picnic at Cactus Canyon!

Story 1 emphasizes:
• two-syllable, short-vowel words and names
• sight words: **for, or, want, too, women**

Bonus Page: Short-Vowel Words with Three or More Syllables

Remember, each syllable has one vowel sound.

Read syllables:	Read words:	Write:	Listen and write:
1. **cab i net**	cabinet	_____	_____
2. **ven i son**	venison	_____	_____
3. **sen ti nel**	sentinel	_____	_____
4. **in hab it**	inhabit	_____	_____
5. **in hib it**	inhibit	_____	_____
6. **ben e fit**	benefit	_____	_____
7. **ba nan as**	bananas	_____	_____
8. **pa ja mas**	pajamas	_____	_____
9. **Ha van a**	Havana	_____	_____
10. **Mon tan a**	Montana	_____	_____
11. **Can a da**	Canada	_____	_____
12. **Pan a ma**	Panama	_____	_____
13. **A las ka**	Alaska	_____	_____
14. **Al a bam a**	Alabama	_____	_____
15. **bul le tin**	bulletin	_____	_____
16. **cat a log**	catalog	_____	_____
17. **im pe tus**	impetus	_____	_____
18. **max i mum**	maximum	_____	_____
19. **min i mum**	minimum	_____	_____
20. **fan tas tic**	fantastic	_____	_____
21. **Ben ja min**	Benjamin	_____	_____

Bonus Page: Sentences Using Short-Vowel Words with Three or More Syllables

Read:

1. Will Benjamin go to Alaska or Panama?
2. Put the venison in the cabinet.
3. The pajamas are in the catalog.
4. They inhabit the cabin in Canada.
5. The jobs have fantastic benefits!
6. Get me seven bananas.
7. Do you want the minimum or the maximum?
8. The bulletin is *The Sentinel.*

Write:

1. _____
2. _____
3. _____
4. _____
5. _____
6. _____
7. _____
8. _____

Listen and write:

1. _____
2. _____
3. _____
4. _____
5. _____
6. _____
7. _____
8. _____

CHAPTER 2:
Nouns and Verbs with Final s and Time-Related Words

In this chapter, you will read, write, compare, and review

► different functions of the final **s**

- verb + **s** = third-person singular verb
- noun + **'s** = possessive noun
- noun + **s** = plural noun

► time-related sight words

- **today**
- **yesterday**
- **was**
- **were**

► sentences and a story that emphasize these lessons

Introduction to Nouns and Verbs

A. NOUN = the name of a person, place, or thing

Read: Write: Read: Write:

a cat   *a cat*   cats   *cats*

an ant   _____   ants   _____

the dog   _____   dogs   _____

the kid   _____   kids   _____

Circle the **noun** in these sentences:

1. The cats sit.   3. The dogs run.

2. The ants dig.   4. The kids nap.

B. VERB = the action that a noun (person or thing) does

Read: Write: Read: Write:

sit   _____   nap   _____

dig   _____   hop   _____

run   _____   sob   _____

Underline the **verb** in these sentences:

1. The cats sit.   3. The dogs run.

2. The ants dig.   4. The kids nap.

CIRCLE the **noun** and underline the **verb** in these sentences:

1. The mitts fit.   7. The bats sip.

2. The men sit.   8   An ax jabs.

3. The kids visit.   9. A van hits.

4. A rat nips.   10. Dads gab.

5. The kin kiss.   11. Moms hug.

6. The bugs hop.   12. The cabs ram.

Sight Words: **today, yesterday**

Today and **yesterday** are words that show present and past time.

For example:

        Today I run.   (present time)

        Yesterday I ran.   (past time)

Read: Today   today   Today   today   Today   today   Today   today

Write: *Today   today* _____

_____

Listen and
write: _____

_____

Read: Yesterday   yesterday   Yesterday   yesterday   Yesterday   yesterday

Write: _____

_____

Listen and
write: _____

_____

COMPARE

Read: Today   today   Yesterday   yesterday   Today   Yesterday   today

          yesterday   Today   Yesterday   today   yesterday   Today   Yesterday

Write: _____

_____

_____

_____

Listen and
write: 1. _____   6. _____

          2. _____   7. _____

          3. _____   8. _____

          4. _____   9. _____

          5. _____   10. _____

Sentences Using **today, yesterday**

Read and compare:

1. Yesterday I fell, so today I am not well.
2. Yesterday you ran to the bus, but today you cannot run.
3. Yesterday her dog had no pep, so today she is at the vet.
4. Yesterday we had no tonic, but today we have some.
5. Yesterday you put ribbons on the hats, and today you can sell them.
6. Yesterday they did fill the cab with gas! Today it is full.

Write:

1. _____

   _____

2. _____

   _____

3. _____

   _____

4. _____

   _____

5. _____

   _____

6. _____

   _____

Listen and write:

1. _____

   _____

2. _____

   _____

3. _____

   _____

Verb Tenses with **today, yesterday**

today (present)	yesterday (past)	today (present)	yesterday (past)
bid	bid	cut	cut
do	did	dig	dug
fit	fit	put	put
hit	hit	bet	bet
quit	quit	let	let
has	had	set	set
run	ran	wed	wed
sit	sat	upset	upset
get	got		

SENTENCES

Use **Today** or **Yesterday** to complete these sentences.   For example:

| _Today_ | he has a tan cab. | (present) |
| _Yesterday_ | he had a red cab. | (past) |

1. _____   you got a rabbit.   (past)

   _____   you can get carrots.   (present)

2. _____   we dug up the hill.   (past)

   _____   we dig up the hill.   (present)

3. _____   they sit on a bus.   (present)

   _____   they sat at the inn.   (past)

Listen and write:

1. _____

2. _____

3. _____

4. _____

5. _____

6. _____

Sight Words: **was, were**
(past tense of the verb **to be**)

Past tense

I was	we were
you were	you were
he was	they were
she was	
it was	

Present tense (review)

I am	we are
you are	you are
he is	they are
she is	
it is	

Read: Write:

1. I was   _____

2. you were   _____

3. he was   _____

4. she was   _____

5. it was   _____

Read: Write:

6. we were   _____

7. you were   _____

8. they **were**   _____

COMPARE

Read: Write:

1. Today I am   _____

    Yesterday I was   _____

2. Today you are   _____

    Yesterday you were   _____

3. Today he is   _____

    Yesterday he was   _____

4. Today she is   _____

    Yesterday she was   _____

5. Today it is   _____

    Yesterday it was   _____

6. Today we are   _____

    Yesterday we were   _____

7. Today they are   _____

    Yesterday they were   _____

Sentences Using **was, were**
(past tense of the verb **to be**)

Read and compare:

1.   Today I am upset. Yesterday I was not upset.
2.   Today you are a comic. Yesterday you were sad.
3.   Today he is in the cabin. Yesterday he was in the mill.
4.   Today the cat is well. Yesterday it was not.
5.   Today the exam is at 6 p.m. Yesterday it was at 7 p.m.
6.   Today we are on a jet. Yesterday we were on a wagon.
7.   Today they are in a cab. Yesterday they were on a bus.

Write:

1.   *Today I am upset.*
     Yesterday I was not upset.

2.   _____

     _____

3.   _____

     _____

4.   _____

     _____

5.   _____

     _____

6.   _____

     _____

7.   _____

     _____

Listen and write:

1.   _____

     _____

2.   _____

     _____

Verb + s = Third-Person Singular

SINGULAR

Read: Write:

1.   I run   _____

2.   you run   _____

3.   he runs   _____

     she runs   _____

     it runs   _____

1.   I sit   _____

2.   you sit   _____

3.   he sits   _____

     she sits   _____

     it sits   _____

1.   I get   _____

2.   you get   _____

3.   he gets   _____

     she gets   _____

     it gets   _____

PLURAL

Read: Write:

1.   we run   _____

2.   you run   _____

3.   they run   _____

1.   we sit   _____

2.   you sit   _____

3.   they sit   _____

1.   we get   _____

2.   you get   _____

3.   they get   _____

Listen and write:

1. _____   7. _____   13. _____

2. _____   8. _____   14. _____

3. _____   9. _____   15. _____

4. _____   10. _____   16. _____

5. _____   11. _____   17. _____

6. _____   12. _____   18. _____

Verbs with and without **s**

Read:	Write:	Read:	Write:
1. I run	I run	he runs	he runs
2. you sit		she sit**s**	
3. we get		it get**s**	
4. they dig		he dig**s**	
5. I fit		she fit**s**	
6. you fill		it fill**s**	
7. we give		he give**s**	
8. they hit		she hit**s**	
9. I live		it live**s**	
10. you pin		he pin**s**	
11. we sip		she sip**s**	
12. they win		it win**s**	
13. I bat		he bat**s**	
14. you lag		she lag**s**	
15. we map		it map**s**	
16. they nap		he nap**s**	
17. I pat		she pat**s**	
18. you mop		it mop**s**	
19. we pass*		he pass**es**	
20. they sass*		she sass**es**	
21. I confess*		it confess**es**	
22. you discuss*		he discuss**es**	
23. we dismiss*		she dismiss**es**	
24. they fix*		it fix**es**	

*When a word ends with the **s** sound, add **es** for the third-person singular.

Listen and write:

1. *I run*

2. *he runs*

3. _____

4. _____

5. _____

6. _____

7. _____

8. _____

9. _____

10. _____

11. _____

12. _____

13. _____

14. _____

15. _____

16. _____

17. _____

18. _____

19. _____

20. _____

21. _____

22. _____

23. _____

24. _____

25. _____

26. _____

27. _____

28. _____

29. _____

30. _____

31. _____

32. _____

33. _____

34. _____

35. _____

36. _____

37. _____

38. _____

39. _____

40. _____

41. _____

42. _____

43. _____

44. _____

45. _____

46. _____

47. _____

48. _____

49. _____

50. _____

Sentences Using Verbs with and without **s**

Read and compare the same verb with different endings:

1.   I **get** a basket, and he **gets** a bag.
2.   You **cut** the melon, and she **cuts** the lemons.
3.   We **sit** in the van, and she **sits** in the wagon.
4.   They **visit** his mom, and he **visits** his dad.

Write:

1.   _____

2.   _____

3.   _____

4.   _____

Read and compare different verbs with different endings:

1.   I **hem** the bottoms, and he **pins** the tops.
2.   You **rub** the cups, and she **buffs** the pots.
3.   We **fix** the clock, and it **runs** well.
4.   They **yell** at the kid, and she **tells** her dad.

Write:

1.   _____

2.   _____

3.   _____

4.   _____

Listen and write:

1.   _____

2.   _____

3.   _____

4.   _____

Noun + 's = Possessive

A. For singular nouns, add 's to show possession.

For example:

Karen   dog   = Karen's dog

Read and write:

1. Karen

   Karen

2. the man

   _____

3. a kitten

   _____

4. the cabin

   _____

5. a bandit

   _____

6. the cactus

   _____

Karen's

Karen's

the man's

_____

a kitten's

_____

the cabin's

_____

a bandit's

_____

the cactus's

_____

Karen's dog

Karen's dog

the man's wagon

_____

a kitten's basket

_____

the cabin's attic

_____

a bandit's bullet

_____

the cactus's pot

_____

B. For plural nouns already ending in s, just add '.

7. the kids

   _____

the kids'

_____

the kids' pets

_____

C. For plural nouns that do not end in s, add 's.

8. the women

   _____

the women's

_____

the women's vans

_____

Listen and write:

1. _____   5. _____

2. _____   6. _____

3. _____   7. _____

4. _____   8. _____

Sentences with 's

Read:

1. Karen's dog is tan and black.
2. The man's wagon is full.
3. A kitten's basket is not big.
4. Go into the cabin's attic.
5. A bandit's bullet hit the hubcap.
6. The cactus's pot is yellow.
7. Do the kids' pets have mats?
8. The women's vans have hubcaps.

Write:

1. _____
2. _____
3. _____
4. _____
5. _____
6. _____
7. _____
8. _____

Listen and write:

1. _____
2. _____
3. _____
4. _____
5. _____
6. _____
7. _____
8. _____

Review: Final s

Singular (noun)	Plural (noun + s)	Possessive (noun + 's)	Third-Person Singular (verb + s)
one dog	seven dogs	the dog's basket	The dog runs.
one rabbit	six rabbits	the rabbit's box	The rabbit hops.

A. NOUNS—SINGULAR AND PLURAL

Read and write each phrase. Add **s,** if necessary, to the underlined word.

Read: Say and write:

1. one melon   *one melon* _____

2. two hubcap   _____

3. three lemon   _____

4. four cabin   _____

5. five napkin   _____

6. a camel   _____

7. six hen   _____

8. seven bandit   _____

9. eight wagon   _____

10. nine salad   _____

11. ten muffin   _____

12. an attic   _____

Listen and write:

1. _____   7. _____

2. _____   8. _____

3. _____   9. _____

4. _____   10. _____

5. _____   11. _____

6. _____   12. _____

B. NOUNS—POSSESSIVE

Read and write each phrase.   Add **'s** or **'** to the underlined word.

Read: Say and write:

1. the <u>dog</u> leg   <u>the dog's leg</u>

2. the <u>basket</u> ribbon   _____

3. the <u>pens</u> tips   _____

4. a <u>man</u> hat   _____

5. <u>Janet</u> doll   _____

6. the <u>caftan</u> button   _____

7. <u>Adam</u> lesson   _____

8. A <u>hen</u> egg   _____

9. the <u>kid</u> tonsils   _____

10. a <u>cactus</u> pot   _____

11. Mrs. <u>Wilson</u> job   _____

12. <u>Dennis</u> exam   _____

Listen and write:

1. _____   7. _____

2. _____   8. _____

3. _____   9. _____

4. _____   10. _____

5. _____   11. _____

6. _____   12. _____

C. VERBS

Read and write each phrase.   Add **s**, if necessary, to the underlined word.

Read: Say and write:

1. I <u>visit</u>   _____

2. you <u>quit</u>   _____

3. he <u>jog</u>   _____

4. she <u>cut</u>   _____

5. it <u>happen</u>   _____

6. we <u>upset</u>   _____

7. you <u>win</u>   _____

8. they <u>sell</u>   _____

9. you and I <u>exit</u>   _____

10. He and she <u>sublet</u> _____

D. NOUNS AND VERBS—SINGULAR AND PLURAL

Choose the correct word to complete each sentence.   Write it in the blank.

1. One rabbit hops_____.   (hop, hops)

2. Two _____ hop.   (rabbit, rabbits)

3. One _____ runs.   (dog, dogs)

4. Three dogs _____.   (run, runs)

5. One camel _____.   (pull, pulls)

6. Four _____ pull.   (camel, camels)

7. Five cats _____.   (tug, tugs)

8. One _____ tugs.   (cat, cats)

9. A kitten _____.   (tug, tugs)

Story 2

Read: **Helen's Lesson**

Today, Helen is jobless. She did not quit. Yesterday, Helen's boss, Mrs.   **1**
Wilson, did dismiss her. Helen was let go. Helen's antics on the job were bad, and she
did not pass her exams on campus.

Mrs. Wilson was upset. She was mad at Helen. Mrs. Wilson said to Helen,   **2**
"You cannot add. You cannot do sums. You sass me, too, and tell me off. Men and
women do not do that on the job. They *cannot* do that on the job! I have had it with
you! You have a lot of talent, Helen, but it is hidden. Go to the campus and get on
with the lessons. Discuss this job with some women and men on campus. Get some
input. If you pass the exam, and if you will not be willful and fitful and a misfit, you
can have the job."

Jobless, Helen cannot sublet the attic she lives in. She gives it up. She has to   **2**
go and live with her mom and dad. She has to confess to them that her job is a loss.

She wells up with sadness and wants to dispel the antics that have gotten her into this mishap. Her dad and mom are upset, too. They tell Helen to get on with her lessons and do well. This impels Helen to do her lessons and to pass her exams.

Helen's exam is on campus today. It is a big exam, too, not a quiz. She had a quiz yesterday. On the exam, Helen has to add some sums. She comes to the exam with pens and a big white tablet.   **4**

The exam upsets Helen. She panics. "Will they expel me?" She wants to vomit, but quells it. She wants to run to the exit and go. Will she? No, she combats her sudden panic. Helen said, "This cannot happen. I will pass! I have to pass or I will not have a job! I have had a lesson." Her panic lessens. Helen passes the exam.   **5**

Helen visits Mrs. Wilson. Mrs. Wilson tells Helen, "You *were* a misfit yesterday, but you are not a misfit today. You have had a big lesson, and you did pass the exam. I have this job for you. You can have it, Helen! If you want, you can go on with the lessons and exams at the campus, too. You have talent with no limit, and you will do well!"   **6**

Story 2 emphasizes:
- verb + **s** (third-person singular)
- noun + **'s** (possessive)
- sight words: **today, yesterday, was, were**

and includes selections from:
- two-syllable, short-vowel words and names
- sight words **for, or, want, too, women**

CHAPTER 3:
Special Sounds

In this chapter, you will learn about special combinations of letters that make one new sound.   You will read, write, compare, and review words with the special sounds.

► **ck** = **k** (final only)

► **sh**

► **ch**

► **tch** (final only)

► **th** (using throat)

► **th** (no throat)

► **wh**

► **ce, ci**

► **ge, gi**

► **dge** (final only)

You also will read and write sentences and stories that emphasize these lessons and contain some words with three or more syllables.

Sound: **ck** = k

lock

Read: ck   ck   ck   ck   ck   ck   ck   ck   ck   ck

Write: C k _____

Listen and
write: _____

COMPARE

Read: ck   c   ck   ck   c   ck   ck   c   k   ck   c   k

ck   k   ck   ck   ck   c   k   ck   c   k   ck   k   ck

Write: _____

Listen and
write: _____

WORDS

(**ck** is found only at the end of a word or syllable)

Read: Write: Read: Write:

1. lock   _____   7. sick   _____

2. back   _____   8. Dick   _____

3. pack   _____   9. sock   _____

4. sack   _____   10. rock   _____

5. neck   _____   11. luck   _____

6. pick   _____   12. duck   _____

Listen and write:

1. _____   5. _____   9. _____

2. _____   6. _____   10. _____

3. _____   7. _____   11. _____

4. _____   8. _____   12. _____

Sentences Using Words with the **ck** = k Sound

Additional words with **ck**:

ack	eck	ick		ock		uck
hack	beck	hick	quick	cock	pocket	buck
Jack	deck	kick	quicken	dock	rocket	muck
lack	beckon	lick	quickness	hock	socket	puck
rack	reckon	Mick	sickness	jock	haddock *	suck
tack	feckless	Nick	gimmick	mock		tuck
unpack	reckless	Rick	picket	pock		bucket
racket		tick	ticktock	docket		luckless
backpack		wick		locket		rucksack

*This is a sight word; see Appendix A.

Read:

1. The duck's neck is green.
2. If she picks the lock, they will lock her up!
3. Pack the socks in the tan sack, too.
4. Were you with Mick yesterday? No, I was sick.
5. Dick had bad luck and fell off his deck.
6. Rick was reckless and hit his back on a rock.

Write:

1. _____
2. _____
3. _____
4. _____
5. _____
6. _____

Listen and write:

1. _____
2. _____
3. _____

Sound: **sh**

ship

Read: sh   s   h   sh   s   h   sh   s   h   sh   s   h   sh   s

Write: sh _____

Listen and
write: _____

COMPARE

Read: sh   s   h   sh   s   h   sh   s   h   sh   s   h   sh   s
         sh   sh   sh   sh   sh   s   h   sh   s   h   sh   s   h   sh

Write: _____

Listen and
write: _____

         _____

WORDS

(**sh** is found at the beginning and end of a word or syllable)

Read: Write: Read: Write:

1. **sh**ip   _____   7. **sh**ut   _____

2. **sh**ed   _____   8. ca**sh**   _____

3. **sh**all   _____   9. ga**sh**   _____

4. **sh**ell   _____   10. di**sh**   _____

5. **sh**in   _____   11. fi**sh**   _____

6. **sh**op   _____   12. ru**sh**   _____

Listen and write:

1. _____   4. _____   7. _____   10. _____

2. _____   5. _____   8. _____   11. _____

3. _____   6. _____   9. _____   12. _____

Sentences Using Words with the **sh** Sound

Additional words with **sh**:

sha/ash	she/esh	shi/ish	sho/osh	shu/ush
sha**ck**	**Sh**ep	cat**fish**	**sh**od	**sh**uck
shad	**sh**ellfish	cod**fish**	**sh**ock	**sh**un
shag	**sh**ellshock	wi**sh**	**sh**ot	
sham			**sh**ellshock	gu**sh**
	me**sh**		big**sh**ot	hu**sh**
a**sh**				lu**sh**
ba**sh**			go**sh**	mu**sh**
da**sh**			po**sh**	
ha**sh**				pu**sh** *
la**sh**				bu**sh** *
ma**sh**				
ra**sh**				
sa**sh**				

*Sight word

Read:

1. Do you want your fish in this dish?
2. Yesterday her shop was shut until seven o'clock.
3. Ship the full box of shells to her.
4. He hid his cash in the shed.
5. Shall I rush and do it?
6. Did she get a gash on her shins?

Write:

1. _____
2. _____
3. _____
4. _____
5. _____
6. _____

Listen and write:

1. _____
2. _____

Sound: ch

check

Read: ch   ch   ch   ch   ch   ch   ch   ch   ch   ch   ch   ch

Write: c h _____

Listen and
write: _____

_____

COMPARE

Read: ch   c   h   ch   c   h   ch   ch   h   ch   c   ch   h

ch   ch   ch   ch   c   h   ch   c   h   ch   c   h   ch

Write: _____

Listen and
write: _____

_____

WORDS

(**ch** is found at the beginning and end of a word or syllable)

Read: Write: Read: Write:

1. **ch**eck   _____   7. **ch**um   _____

2. **ch**ap   _____   8. ri**ch**   _____

3. **ch**ill   _____   9. mu**ch**   _____

4. **ch**in   _____   10. su**ch**   _____

5. **ch**ip   _____   11. ben**ch**   _____

6. **ch**op   _____   12. lun**ch**   _____

Listen and write:

1. _____   4. _____   7. _____   10. _____

2. _____   5. _____   8. _____   11. _____

3. _____   6. _____   9. _____   12. _____

Sentences Using Words with the **ch** Sound

Additional words with **ch**:

cha	che/ench	chi	cho	chu/unch
Chad	**Ch**en	**ch**ick	**ch**ock	**ch**ug
chaff	**ch**ess	**Ch**ip		**ch**uck
Chan	**Ch**et	**ch**it		**Ch**uck
chat		**ch**icken		**ch**uck wagon
	ben**ch**	**ch**itlins		
	hen**ch**man	**ch**in-up		mun**ch**
				pun**ch**
				lun**ch** box

Read:

1. Chan did chop a lot of logs!
2. Chen put some chips in a box on the bench.
3, Chet will chill the chicken.
4. Will his chum, Chad, get the lunch today?
5. Did the wet sand chap her chin?
6. Chuck is such a rich man! He has lots of checks.

Write:

1. _____
2. _____
3. _____
4. _____
5. _____
6. _____

Listen and write:

1. _____
2. _____
3. _____

Sound: **tch** = **ch**

match

Read: tch   tch   tch   tch   tch   tch   tch   tch   tch

Write: _____

Listen and
write: _____

COMPARE

Read: tch   tch   ch   ch   ch   tch   ch   tch   ch   ch   ch   tch
        tch   tch   tch   tch   ch   ch   tch   tch   ch   tch   ch   tch

Write: _____

Listen and
write: _____

      _____

WORDS

(**tch** is found only at the end of a word or syllable)

Read: Write: Read: Write:

1. ma**tch**   _____   7. pi**tch**   _____

2. ca**tch**   _____   8. la**tch**   _____

3. di**tch**   _____   9. ba**tch**   _____

4. fe**tch**   _____   10. Mi**tch**   _____

5. ha**tch**   _____   11. no**tch**   _____

6. hi**tch**   _____   12. hu**tch**   _____

Listen and write:

1. _____   4. _____   7. _____   10. _____

2. _____   5. _____   8. _____   11. _____

3. _____   6. _____   9. _____   12. _____

Sentences Using Words with the **tch** = ch Sound

Additional words with **tch**:

atch	etch	itch	otch	utch
patch	**etch**	**itch**	**botch**	Dutch
unlatch	**retch**	**Mitch**ell		
hatchback				**Butch***

*Sight word

Read:

1. If Donna will pitch, Dennis will catch.
2. Mitch cut a notch in the log.
3. Was the latch hidden on that hatch?
4. I want to fetch the dog and hitch it to the wagon.
5. A batch of muffins is in the oven.
6. Match a bench to the Dutch hutch.

Write:

1. _____
2. _____
3. _____
4. _____
5. _____
6. _____

Listen and write:

1. _____
2. _____
3. _____
4. _____
5. _____
6. _____

Review: Words with **ck, ch, tch, sh**

1. Read **ch** and **tch.** Hear the same sound.

    ch tch ch tch ch tch ch tch ch tch ch tch

    Read: Write:

    chop   su**ch**   ma**tch**   _____ _____ _____

    chin   mu**ch**   pi**tch**   _____ _____ _____

2. Read **ch, tch,** and **sh.** Hear that **sh** makes a different sound.

    ch tch sh ch tch sh ch tch sh ch tch sh

    Read (beginnings):   Write:

    chip   **sh**ip   _____ _____

    chop   **sh**op   _____ _____

    chum   **sh**ut   _____ _____

    chat   **sh**all   _____ _____

    Read (endings):   Write:

    ba**tch**   ba**sh**   _____ _____

    di**tch**   di**sh**   _____ _____

    mu**ch**   mu**sh**   _____ _____

3. Read **ch, tch,** and **ck.** Hear that **ck** makes a different sound.

    ch tch ck ch tch ck ch tch ck ch tch ck

    Read: Write:

    pa**ck**   pa**tch**   _____ _____

    pi**ck**   pi**tch**   _____ _____

    su**ck**   su**ch**   _____ _____

    mu**ck**   mu**ch**   _____ _____

Listen and write:

1. _____
2. _____
3. _____
4. _____
5. _____
6. _____
7. _____
8. _____
9. _____
10. _____
11. _____
12. _____
13. _____
14. _____
15. _____
16. _____
17. _____
18. _____
19. _____
20. _____

21. _____
22. _____
23. _____
24. _____
25. _____
26. _____
27. _____
28. _____
29. _____
30. _____
31. _____
32. _____
33. _____
34. _____
35. _____
36. _____
37. _____
38. _____
39. _____
40. _____

41. _____
42. _____
43. _____
44. _____
45. _____
46. _____
47. _____
48. _____
49. _____
50. _____
51. _____
52. _____
53. _____
54. _____
55. _____
56. _____
57. _____
58. _____
59. _____
60. _____

Review: Sentences with **ck**, **ch**, **tch**, **sh**

Read:

1. I lit the wick with the match.
2. Rush and shut the ship's hatch!
3. A codfish has no shell.
4. Chuck wants to cash his check today.
5. She and Mitch were sick of chess.
6. Shuck that batch of shellfish on the deck.
7. Can Shep fetch the lunch for us?

Write:

1. _____
2. _____
3. _____
4. _____
5. _____
6. _____
7. _____

Listen and write:

1. _____
2. _____
3. _____
4. _____
5. _____
6. _____
7. _____

Story 3

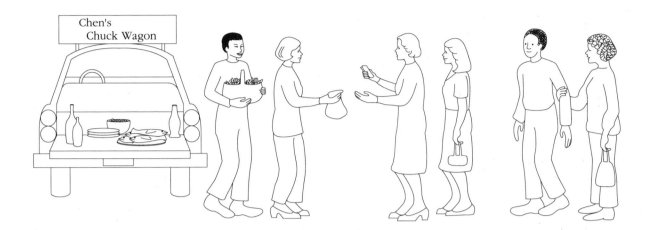

Read: **Chen's Chuck Wagon**

Chen has a lunch shop in his hatchback. It is *CHEN'S CHUCK WAGON*. He **1** sells fish and chips for lunch. He has catfish, codfish, haddock, shad, bass, and shellfish on buns. Chen sells tonic, punch, and salad, too. This is his job. He wants to do well and get rich. With his talent and some luck, he will.

At sunup, Chen picks up Hanna. She is his chum. It is her job to go with Chen **2** to the docks, so they can fetch a batch of fish. They will get today's catch of fish off the ships. Chen gives a big check for his fish. It is a lot of bucks! Chen is mad to give so much, but Hanna pats him on the back.

"Do not be upset," she tells Chen. "We will go to the Mitchell Jacket Shop and **3** sell this fish for lunch. Then you will get lots of cash."

Chen peps up. "Hanna, you are such a chum!" **4**

With Chen's fish, the chums go into a rustic shed on the dock. It is an unfit **5** shack full of shells, but they have to sublet it to cut and chop the fish. They have had mishaps in the shack. Yesterday it was wet in the shack, and Hanna fell and cut her chin on a shell chip. Chen fell and got a gash on his shin. They get a chill in the shack, too. Today they have jackets on and will check for wet shell chips in the shed.

The pals unpack the fish and discuss the uncut catch. Hanna shucks the **6** shellfish. Chen cuts and chops the catfish, shad, bass, and codfish. It is such a mess, but they have fun, too! They put the fish in the oven until it is hot and brown. Then they put the fish in Chen's hatchback. They rush to put in the buns and the chips. Chen has seven gallons of lemon tonic and ten big salads in a rucksack. They chill the punch. Hanna has the cups, napkins, and dishes in her backpack. They put that in, too. The hatchback is chock full! *CHEN'S CHUCK WAGON* is set for lunch. The chums lock the latch and dash off to the Mitchell Jacket Shop to sell the lunch.

At the Mitchell Jacket Shop, the jobs are to cut, hem, and tack jackets. Lots of   **7**
men and women are on the job. They put patch pockets on jackets. They match socks and sashes to the jackets, and put them in packets to sell. They do shag rugs and mesh bags, too. Mitchell's is not a posh or lush shop.

At 11:45 a.m., Chen and Hanna are at Mitchell's. "Come and get it!" yells   **8**
Chen. "Be quick, for it is hot!" yells Hanna.

The men and women rush to *CHEN'S CHUCK WAGON* in bunches. Some   **9**
want salad and tonic. Some itch for fish and chips. Some want lots of dishes, napkins, and cups. Some have a lunch box and sit on a bench. For some, chess is a habit at lunch; they sit in the sun with a chess set on a rock. Some women and men munch and chat with Hanna and Chen. Some do not chat. They want to pack it in until they are full and go back to the job.

"Do you have hash or chicken and chitlins? Do you have hot dogs?" a man   **10**
yells.

"Not today," yells Chen, "but we do have shad, catfish, and haddock."   **11**

A woman yells, "Did you chill the punch today?"   **12**

"Gosh, yes!" Chen yells back.   **13**

At 1 p.m., the women and men go back to the jobs at Mitchell's. Hanna and   **14**
Chen pick up the mess, pack it up, and toss it into a bucket. They put the bucket in the hatchback, and lock up *CHEN'S CHUCK WAGON*.

"Chen, did you get much cash today?"   **15**

"Yes, Hanna, we were in luck! I did get a lot today. And I have a big check for   **16**
you. With you as a chum, I am rich!"

Story 3 emphasizes:
- special sounds: **ck, sh, ch, tch**

and includes selections from:
- two-syllable, short-vowel words and names
- verb + **s** (third-person singular); noun + **'s** (possessive)
- sight words: **for, or, want, too, women, today, yesterday, was, were**

Sound: **th**   **the**

Use your throat to make this sound: **th**

Read: th   th   th   th   th   th   th   th   th   th

Write: t h _____

Listen and
write: _____

COMPARE

Read: th   t   h   th   t   h   th   t   h   th   t   h   th   t

            th   th   th   th   t   h   th   t   h   th   t   h   th

Write: _____

                 _____

Listen and
write: _____

                 _____

WORDS

Read: Write: Read: Write:

1. **th**e   _____   5. **th**en   _____

2. **th**is   _____   6. **th**em   _____

3. **th**at   _____   7. **th**ey*   _____

4. **th**an   _____   8. **th**us   _____

Listen and write:

1. _____   4. _____   7. _____   10. _____

2. _____   5. _____   8. _____   11. _____

3. _____   6. _____   9. _____   12. _____

*sight word

Sentences Using Words with the **th** Sound

Remember to use your throat to make this sound.

Read:

1. Chop the codfish, then put it into the wagon.
2. Did they discuss that exam?
3. This van is a hatchback, but that van is not.
4. They fix bags, so give them to them.
5. This check was less than that check.
6. Put it in that basket, not in this dish.
7. They have no cash; thus, they have to get a job.

Write:

1. _____
2. _____
3. _____
4. _____
5. _____
6. _____
7. _____

Listen and write:

1. _____
2. _____
3. _____
4. _____
5. _____
6. _____
7. _____

Sound: **th**

 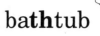

Use your teeth and tongue only (no throat) to make this sound.

Read: th   th   th   th   th   th   th   th   th   th

Write: t h _____

Listen and
write: _____

COMPARE

Read: th   h   th   t   th   t   th   h   th   h   th   t   th
        th   th   th   th   t   h   th   t   h   th   t   h   th

Write: _____

Listen and
write: _____

        _____

WORDS

Read: Write: Read: Write:

1.   ba**th**   _____   7.   Se**th**   _____

2.   **th**ick   _____   8.   me**th**od   _____

3.   **th**in   _____   9.   **th**ing*   _____

4.   ma**th**   _____   10. no**th**ing*   _____

5.   wi**th**   _____   11. **th**ink*   _____

6.   Be**th**   _____   12. **th**ank*   _____

*sight word

Listen and write:

1. _____   4. _____   7. _____   10. _____

2. _____   5. _____   8. _____   11. _____

3. _____   6. _____   9. _____   12. _____

Sentences Using Words with the **th** Sound

Remember to use your teeth and tongue only (no throat) to make this sound.
Additional words with **th**:

pa**th**	**th**icket	**th**ud
ki**th**	**th**icken	**Th**elma
ba**th**tub	**th**ickness	Be**th**lehem
wi**th**in	**th**ickset	mon**th***
		some**th**ing*

*****o = ŭ** (sun)

Read:

1. At the picnic this month, Beth was with Seth.
2. Thelma got you that wagon. Did you thank her?
3. They think Karen is thin, but she thinks she is fat!
4. She has seven things, but he has nothing.
5. This kid has lots of fun in the bathtub.
6. Today, I think the math lesson has a method to it.

Write:

1. _____
2. _____
3. _____
4. _____
5. _____
6. _____

Listen and write:

1. _____
2. _____
3. _____
4. _____
5. _____

Sound: **wh**

whip

Feel your breath as you make this sound.

Read: wh   wh   wh   wh   wh   wh   wh   wh   wh   wh

Write: Wh _____

Listen and
write: _____

COMPARE

Read: wh   w   h   wh   w   h   wh   h   h   w   w   h   wh   w

wh   wh   wh   wh   w   h   wh   w   h   wh   w   h   wh

Write: _____

_____

Listen and
write: _____

_____

WORDS

Read: Write: Read: Write:

1. **wh**ip   _____   6. **wh**am   _____

2. **wh**en   _____   7. **wh**im   _____

3. **wh**ich   _____   8. **wh**iff   _____

4. **wh**iz   _____   9. **wh**at*   _____

5. **wh**ack   10. **wh**ite   _____

*sight word

Listen and write:

1. _____   4. _____   7. _____   10. _____

2. _____   5. _____   8. _____   11. _____

3. _____   6. _____   9. _____   12. _____

Sentences Using Words with the **wh** Sound

Compare the sound of **wh** with **w**.

Additional words with **wh**:

whet	**wh**isk	**wh**op
	whit	

Read:

1. He whacks the log with an ax. Wham!
2. Yesterday that white wig was big. Today it fits!
3. Yes, Max is a willful kid, but he is a whiz at math.
4. Which dog whips into the den?
5. When he gets a whiff of lunch, he runs to get some.
6. Do I whisk or whip the egg whites?

Write:

1. _____
2. _____
3. _____
4. _____
5. _____
6. _____

Listen and write:

1. _____
2. _____
3. _____
4. _____
5. _____
6. _____

Sound: c = s
(before **e** and **i**)

c**e**nt   pen**ci**l

Read: | ce | ce | ce | ce | ce | ce | ci | ci | ci | ci | ci

Write: c e _____

Listen and
write: _____

COMPARE

Note the difference between the hard sounds **că**, **cŏ**, **cŭ** (**ca**t, **co**t, **cu**t) and the soft sounds
cĕ, **cĭ** (**ce**nt, pen**ci**l).

Read: ce se ci si ce ci ce ci se si ce ci
        ca co cu ce ci ca ce ci co cu ce ci

Write: _____

Listen and
write: _____

_____

WORDS

Read: Write:

1. **c**ent   _____

2. pen**ci**l   _____

3. **c**ell   _____

4. fen**ce**   _____

5. sin**ce**   _____

6. dan**ce**   _____

Read: Write:

7. Ali**ce**   _____

8. **ce**nsus   _____

9. min**ce**   _____

10. **ci**vic   _____

11. **ci**tizen   _____

12. **Ce**ci**l**   _____

Listen and write:

1. _____   4. _____   7. _____   10. _____

2. _____   5. _____   8. _____   11. _____

3. _____   6. _____   9. _____   12. _____

Comparing and Contrasting Words with **ce, ci, ca, co, cu**

1. Read the words in the **ce, ci** chart. Note that in these words **ce** and **ci** have a soft sound like **s**.

2. Circle the **ce** or **ci** in each word.

3. Find the word with both **ce** and **ci** and underline it. It is listed twice.

Words with **ce, ci** (soft sound like **s**):

ce			ci	
Alice	fence	office	acid	citrus
cancel	hence	pence	Cecil	civet
Cecil	incense	sentence	cinch	civic
cell	justice	since	cinema	civil
census	lance	success	cinnamon	illicit
cent	lettuce	thence	citadel	pencil
chance	malice	whence	citizen	rancid
dance	mince	wince	citron	solicit
excel	ocelot			

4. Read the words in the **ca, co, cu** chart. Note that in these words **ca, co,** and **cu** have a hard sound like **k**.

5. Circle the **ca, co,** or **cu** in each word.

6. Find the word that is on the **ca, co, cu** chart that is also on the **ce, ci** chart. Underline this word on both charts.

Words with **ca, co,** and **cu** (hard sound like **k**):

ca		co		cu
cabin	cannon	cob	commit	cup
cactus	cannot	cod	compel	cuspid
caftan	canyon	coffin	confess	custom
Calvin	carat	colic	Conrad	cut
camel	caravan	combat	cop	cutlet
cancel	carrot	comet	cotton	cutoff
candid	catnip	comic		cutup

Sentences: Comparing and Contrasting Words with Hard and Soft **c**

Read:

1. The carrot and cactus are ten cents.
2. Did Calvin have a chance to dance with Alice?
3. The census office cannot tax citizens.
4. Since the sentence is in pencil, I can fix it.
5. It is her custom to mince cinnamon in that cup.
6. The cops can put them into a cell until they confess. Is this justice?

Write:

1. _____
2. _____
3. _____
4. _____
5. _____
6. _____

Listen and write:

1. _____
2. _____
3. _____
4. _____
5. _____
6. _____

Sound: **g** = j

(before **e** and **i**)

gem 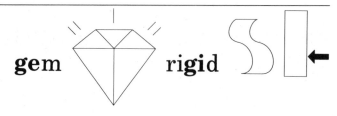 ri**gi**d

Read: ge   ge   ge   ge   gi   gi   gi   gi   ge   gi   ge   gi

Write: ge _____

Listen and
write: _____

COMPARE

Note the difference between the hard sounds **ga**, **go**, **gu** (**ga**p, **go**t, **gu**m), and the soft
sounds **ge**, **gi** (**ge**m, ri**gi**d).

Read: ge   je   gi   ji   ga   go   gu   ge   gi   ga   go   gu
         je   ji   ge   gi   ge   gi   ge   ji   ge   gi   ga   ge

Write: _____

Listen and
write: _____

         _____

WORDS

Read: Write: Read: Write:

1. **ge**m   _____   7. **gi**st   _____

2. ri**gi**d   _____   8. vi**gi**l   _____

3. le**ge**nd   _____   9. **gi**blets   _____

4. **ge**l   _____   10. hin**ge**   _____

5. colle**ge** _____   11. **age**nda   _____

6. **ge**latin _____   12. alle**ge**   _____

Listen and write:

1. _____   4. _____   7. _____   10. _____

2. _____   5. _____   8. _____   11. _____

3. _____   6. _____   9. _____   12. _____

Sentences Using Words with the ge, gi Sounds

Additional words with **ge**, **gi**:

re**gi**men
impin**ge**

Special cases when **ge**, **gi** make a hard sound:

ge	**gi**
get	**gi**ll
	gimmick
	give
	given

Review of the hard **g** sound in **ga**, **go**, **gu**:

ga	**go**	**gu**
gab	**go**b	**gu**ll
gag	**go**t	**gu**m
gal		**gu**n
gap		**Gu**s
gas		**gu**t

Read:

1. Was the college exam on your agenda today?
2. Gus will fix the rigid hinge with a gel.
3. Cut the gab and get back to the job!
4. As the gelatin set, the gals got the giblets.
5. Did you get the gist of that legend?
6. On his vigil, the cop had to lock up the gems.

Write:

1. _____
2. _____
3. _____
4. _____
5. _____
6. _____

Listen and write:

1. _____
2. _____
3. _____
4. _____
5. _____
6. _____

Sound: **dge** = ge, je

ba**dge**

Read: dge   dge   dge   dge   dge   dge   dge   dge   dge   dge

Write: _____

Listen and
write: _____

COMPARE

Read: dge   ge   je   dge   ge   dge   dge   je   dge   dge   ge
        je   dge   ge   je   dge   dge   ge   je   dge   ge   je

Write: _____

Listen and
write: _____

_____

WORDS

Read: Write: Read: Write:

1. ba**dge**   _____   7. do**dge**   _____

2. e**dge**   _____   8. lo**dge**   _____

3. he**dge**   _____   9. bu**dge**   _____

4. le**dge**   _____   10. fu**dge**   _____

5. we**dge**   _____   11. ju**dge**   _____

6. ri**dge**   _____   12. nu**dge**   _____

Listen and write:

1. _____   4. _____   7. _____   10. _____

2. _____   5. _____   8. _____   11. _____

3. _____   6. _____   9. _____   12. _____

Sentences Using Words with the **dge** Sound

Additional words with **dge**:

fi**dge**t	wi**dge**t	ho**dge**po**dge**
bu**dge**t	porri**dge**	he**dge**hog

Word with hard **g** and soft **g**:

ga**dg**et

Read:
1. A cop, not a judge, has a badge.
2. They nudge but cannot budge the rock.
3. A widget is a gadget that is not big.
4. Wedge the pick into the ledge on the ridge.
5. On his budget he can get porridge, but no fudge.
6. The lodge had a hodgepodge of things.
7. At the edge of her hedge, two hedgehogs dodge the dog.

Write:
1. _____
2. _____
3. _____
4. _____
5. _____
   _____
6. _____
7. _____
   _____

Listen and write:
1. _____
2. _____
3. _____
4. _____

Review:
Sentences with **th**, **wh**, **ce**, **ci**, **ge**, **gi**, **dge**

Read:

1. Seth's budget let him get a white bathtub for the lodge.
2. Since this judge is so rigid, will Beth get justice with her?
3. Thelma fidgets and winces when she cannot get the gist of a dance method.
4. At the office, Cecil fell with a thud, then he did not budge.
5. That job hinges on his success with math and civics at college.
6. Nothing fell off the edge of the fence, thus nothing cut the hedge.
7. At the Dodge Civic Lodge today, the citizens want a chance to discuss the agenda.
8. It is a cinch to whip the gelatin, mince the lemon, and put them on a wedge of lettuce.

Write:

1. _____

_____

2. _____

_____

3. _____

_____

4. _____

_____

5. _____

_____

6. _____

_____

7. _____

_____

8. _____

_____

Listen and write:

1. _____

_____

2. _____

_____

2. _____

_____

4. _____

_____

5. _____

_____

6. _____

_____

7. _____

_____

8. _____

_____

9. _____

_____

10. _____

_____

11. _____

_____

12. _____

_____

13. _____

_____

14. _____

_____

15. _____

Special Skill
PREVIEWING WORDS OF THREE OR MORE SYLLABLES
FROM THE STORY Justice Comes to Ridgeton

Remember that each syllable has one vowel sound.

Read syllables:	Read words:	Write the words:
1. a gen da	agenda	*agenda*
2. al le ges	alleges	
3. ben e fit	benefit	
4. cab i net	cabinet	
5. cit i zens	citizens	
6. il lic it	illicit	
7. max i mum	maximum	
8. min i mum	minimum	
9. sen ten ces	sentences	
10. so lic it	solicit	
11. wit ness es	witnesses	

Listen and write:

1. _____   7. _____

2. _____   8. _____

3. _____   9. _____

4. _____   10. _____

5. _____   11. _____

6. _____   12. _____

Story 4

Read: **Justice Comes to Ridgeton**

Today is a big day in Ridgeton. Judge Alice G. Dodge will be on the bench.   **1**
Judge Dodge is something of a legend, since she has a lot of wisdom and is not rigid.
The public can come, so citizens jam-pack the benches. They wedge in and nudge and
push and will not budge. Women and men of the college have come, too, for a civics
lesson. They are a big mob!

Some cops with badges and guns are at vigil at the edge of the mob. The cops   **2**
have an office and cells in Ridgeton, too. In the office is a cabinet with a big lock on
it. Racks of guns, boxes of bullets, and cuffs for felons are in the cabinet.

Judge Dodge sits on the bench, in black, with today's docket, her gavel, pencils,   **3**
and pens. With Judge Dodge, 12 men and women sit in a box. They are on the public
census. They discuss what the witnesses said and tell the judge what they think.
Then the judge passes sentence. A witness is in the witness box.

Men, women, and kids will come up to the bench. Some are not too bad, but   **4**
some are felons. The docket is full today, and the judge has a big agenda:

1. **Kids hit bus with rocks and buckshot**
2. **Man picks lock on hatchback**
3. **Bandits rob Whitman's Gem Shop**
4. **Ridgeton citizen reckless with cab; victim gets whiplash**
5. **Hit man gets ransom, kills rich kidnap victim**

What will the kids, women, and men on the docket tell the judge?
What will the witnesses in the witness box tell the judge?
Will the 12 men and women in the box tell the judge what they think?
Will the cops tell the judge things, too?

What will Judge Dodge tell them?

Will the judge give some minimum sentences; some maximum sentences?

Will the public benefit? Will Ridgeton get justice?

1. Kids hit bus with rocks and buckshot

Did Dick and Ann Hodge's kids, Beth and Rick, toss rocks at a bus? Yes, men and   **5**
women on the bus were witnesses. They allege that the kids shot buckshot at the bus,
too.

      Judge Dodge said to Beth and Rick, "You did a bad thing, but you are not bad   **6**
kids. This is not a habit and custom for you. You were misled. You are not cutups,
but are in with a bad bunch of kids. I cannot let you off, but I shall not commit you to
cells. I want you to do a job at the Ridgeton Kids' Lodge. If you do the job well, I will
do what I can for you. I want you to get some chums that are not bad, too."

      "Beth, since you are a chess whiz, do that with some of the kids at the Lodge.   **7**
Rick, since you are a math whiz, do math with them. You can fence and dance with
them, too. In four months, Dr. Hatch of the Lodge will tell me if you did the jobs well.
This sentence hinges on this job. Then, if you and Dr. Hatch want, you can get a job
for cash at the Lodge."

      Judge Dodge then said, "Mr. and Mrs. Hodge, come up to the bench and be   **8**
with Beth and Rick. I want you to discuss things with the kids. Give them things to
do and do things with them."

      Mrs. Hodge said, "Thank you, Judge, for this chance. We will do that."   **9**

      Rick and Beth said to Judge Dodge, "Thanks a lot. We will do what you said   **10**
with the kids at the Lodge for four months, and we will discuss things with Mom and
Dad, too."

2. Man picks lock on hatchback

Did Chuck Cecil pick the lock on Seth Hicks's hatchback? Yes, Miss Linda Chen was   **11**
a witness. She alleges that Mr. Cecil did pick it. Miss Chen got the cops, and they got
him.

      Judge Dodge said to Chuck Cecil, "I shall pass sentence on you, Mr. Cecil. I   **12**
commit you to 30 days in a cell. This is the minimum. But you can lessen this
sentence, too, if you do some civic job to benefit the citizens of Ridgeton. You are civil,
and you are candid with me. Sit in the cell and think of what you can do for the
public. I want you to think of what *you* can do for *you,* too. Get with it, Mr. Cecil! Did
you get the gist of what I said, Mr. Cecil? Tell me today, and I shall do what I can for
you."

"Thank you, Judge Dodge," said Chuck Cecil. "I get the gist of what you **13** said. I will think of some things to do for the public. I will think of things I can do for me, too. Yesterday was bad for me and I had nothing, but today I have a chance."

3. Bandits rob Whitman's Gem Shop

Did Gemma Conrad and Butch Sedgewick rob Whitman's Gem Shop? Yes, they did. The **14** cops cut them off as they ran. Gemma had a gun with her, but it had no bullets in it. The cops got Butch and Gemma, and put cuffs on them. Gemma and Butch had lockets, cash, and gems in a canvas bag. They do not have jobs, and they do not want them. Butch and Gemma want to fence the gems at an illicit hock shop for a quick buck. Butch got a ten-carat rock at Whitman's, too. He put it on Gemma, his chick, and said, "This is for you. I will not fence it." She *did* want it, and *did* kiss Butch for it as they ran.

Three witnesses sat in the box. They allege that Butch and Gemma *did* rob **15** Whitman's. Gemma Conrad and Butch Sedgewick then did confess.

Judge Dodge said, "You cannot be rich if you do not have jobs. Illicit cash will **16** not give you what you want. For the benefit of the public, I pass sentence on you: I commit Butch Sedgewick to 11 months in a cell, but I commit Gemma Conrad to 15 months in a cell. Since you, Ms. Conrad, had a gun with you, the office of judge compels me to give you the maximum sentence. If you give back the 10-carat gem to Whitman's, I can lessen the sentence."

Gemma Conrad did fidget. She was upset, but said, "Yes, I will give the rock **17** back to Whitman's. Thank you, Judge, for the chance."

Judge Dodge said, "I shall get back to you in the cell within ten days. We will **18** visit, and I shall do what I can for you if Whitman's gets the gem."

4. Ridgeton citizen reckless with cab; victim gets whiplash

Was Mrs. Thelma Lodge of Ridgeton reckless? Did she hit Lance Gillett's van with **19** her cab?

Mr. Gillett tells the judge he has whiplash. He winces since his back and neck **20** were hit. When he sits, he is rigid. He cannot sit in the bathtub. He cannot do his job, which is to cut hedges and thickets at the college. In his van, he picks up logs and pulls up decks that are rotten, too. A cop was a witness. She alleges that Mr. Gillett got whiplash when Mrs. Lodge hit the back of his van with her cab.

The judge said to Thelma Lodge, "Give Mr. Gillett a check for his losses, or I **21** will have to commit you to a cell."

Mrs. Lodge said, "Judge Dodge, I will give Lance Gillett a check for his losses." **22**

5. Hit man gets ransom, kills rich kidnap victim

With the cops is a thickset man, a thug, with a thick neck. He thuds up to the bench.   **23**
The cops have guns, and this man is in cuffs. He has a cap on that hid him. The
public fidgets on the benches for he is a big, bad man. He is Mack Maxwell. To his
"chums" in the mob, he is Mad Max, the hit man. He has a gun as big as a cannon.
Did Mack Maxwell kidnap Cedric Whelton, a rich man? Yes! Maxwell hid the cash he
had gotten for Whelton's ransom, but he did not let Whelton go. He put a gag on
Whelton, shot him with seven bullets, and put him into a coffin. Then he had his
henchmen push the coffin off a ledge. Maxwell is a bad man!

When the cops got him, the hit man said with malice, "I will get back at you!"   **24**

Judge Dodge tells the public, "This is Mack (Mad Max) Maxwell. He will get   **25**
his sentence today. He *did* kidnap and kill Cedric Whelton. He got a big ransom. We
have witnesses. They have said what he did."

Cedric Whelton's kith and kin are sad and mad. Some of them sob. They want   **26**
Judge Dodge to "sock it" to Maxwell. They solicit the judge to give him the maximum
sentence.

Judge Dodge said to Mack Maxwell, "You are a bad man, and you did lots of   **27**
bad things. You will not get off today, Mr. Maxwell. Today you will get justice. You
will get the maximum sentence. I will not let the public be victim to you and the
malice you commit!"

Mack (Mad Max) Maxwell said nothing to Judge Dodge. The cops led him to   **28**
his cell.

Justice had come to Ridgeton today.   **29**

Story 4 emphasizes:
- special sounds: **th, wh, ce, ci, ge, gi, dge**

and includes selections from:
- two-syllable, short-vowel words and names
- verb + **s** (third-person singular); noun + **'s** (possessive)
- special sounds: **ck, sh, ch, tch**
- sight words: **for, or, want, too, women, today, yesterday, was, were, thing, something, nothing, think, thank, what**
- three-syllable words: **agenda, alleges, benefit, cabinet, citizens, illicit, maximum, minimum, sentences, solicit, witnesses**

CHAPTER 4:
Blends

In this chapter, you will read, write, compare, and review words with

► initial blends; for example, **fl** (**fl**ag) and **dr** (**dr**op)

► final blends; for example, **ct** (a**ct**) and **mp** (du**mp**)

You also will read and write sentences and stories that emphasize these lessons and contain some words with three or more syllables.

Introduction to Initial Blends

In a blend, two letters (consonants) keep their two sounds but are pronounced very closely together.

Read the short vowels:		ă	ĕ	ĭ	ŏ	ŭ
Read the starting sounds:		la	le	li	lo	lu
Read the consonant before the starting sounds:		b la	b le	b li	b lo	b lu
Read faster, blending the sounds together:		bla	ble	bli	blo	blu

INITIAL BLENDS WITH l

Read the blends and the words: Write the words twice:

black   *black*

1. **b la**   **bla**   **black**
2. **b le**   **ble**   **bled**
3. b li   bli   blip
4. b lo   blo   blot
5. B lu   Blu   Blum

6. c la   cla   class
7. C le   Cle   Clem
8. c li   cli   clip
9. c lo   clo   clock
10. c lu   clu   club

11. f la   fla   flag
12. f le   fle   fled
13. f li   fli   flip
14. f lo   flo   flop
15. f lu   flu   fluff

Read the blends and the words: Write the words twice:

16. g la   gla   glass   _____   _____

17. g le   gle   glen   _____   _____

18. g li   gli   glib   _____   _____

19. g lo   glo   glop   _____   _____

20. g lu   glu   glum   _____   _____

21. p la   pla   plan   _____   _____

22. p li   pli   plink   _____   _____

23. p lo   plo   plop   _____   _____

24. p lu   plu   plum   _____   _____

25. s la   sla   slap   _____   _____

26. s le   sle   sled   _____   _____

27. s li   sli   slip   _____   _____

28. s lo   slo   slop   _____   _____

29. s lu   slu   slum   _____   _____

Listen and write:

1. _____   8. _____   15. _____

2. _____   9. _____   16. _____

3. _____   10. _____   17. _____

4. _____   11. _____   18. _____

5. _____   12. _____   19. _____

6. _____   13. _____   20. _____

7. _____   14. _____   21. _____

More Initial Blends with l
(Including Special Endings: ck, sh, ch, tch, th, wh, ce, ci, ge, gi, dge)

Read: Write:

1. **bla**b   _____
2. **ble**ss _____
3. bliss   _____
4. blob   _____
5. block   _____
6. blotch   _____
7. bluff   _____
8. blur   _____
9. blush   _____
10. clack   _____
11. clad   _____
12. clam   _____
13. clan   _____
14. clap   _____
15. clash   _____
16. clef   _____
17. click   _____
18. cliff   _____
19. clod   _____
20. clog   _____
21. clop   _____
22. clot   _____
23. cluck   _____
24. clutch   _____
25. flab   _____

Read: Write:

26. flack   _____
27. flam   _____
28. flan   _____
29. flap   _____
30. flash   _____
31. flat   _____
32. fleck   _____
33. flesh   _____
34. flex   _____
35. flick   _____
36. flit   _____
37. flog   _____
38. flock   _____
39. flub   _____
40. flush   _____
41. glad   _____
42. glim   _____
43. glob   _____
44. glut   _____
45. pled   _____
46. pledge   _____
47. plod   _____
48. plot   _____
49. pluck   _____
50. plug   _____

Read: Write: Read: Write:

51. plush   _____   61. slim   _____

52. slab   _____   62. slit   _____

53. slack   _____   63. slob   _____

54. slap   _____   64. slog   _____

55. slam   _____   65. slosh   _____

56. slash   _____   66. slot   _____

57. slat   _____   67. sloth   _____

58. sledge   _____   68. sludge   _____

59. slick   _____   69. slug   _____

60. slid   _____   70. slush   _____

Listen and write:

1. _____   13. _____   25. _____

2. _____   14. _____   26. _____

3. _____   15. _____   27. _____

4. _____   16. _____   28. _____

5. _____   17. _____   29. _____

6. _____   18. _____   30. _____

7. _____   19. _____   31. _____

8. _____   20. _____   32. _____

9. _____   21. _____   33. _____

10. _____   22. _____   34. _____

11. _____   23. _____   35. _____

12. _____   24. _____   36. _____

Sentences: Initial Blends with l

Read:

1.   The club has a red and black flag.

2.   Her dog, Fluff, bit Mr. Blum and fled.

3.   Set the class clock to go ticktock.

4.   Clem cut his lip on glass and bled.

5.   That sled will slip and flip.

6.   Did the glop of sap plop on the plum?

7.   Did you pledge cash to the college budget?

8.   He has a plan to fix up that block of slums.

Write:

1.   _____

2.   _____

3.   _____

4.   _____

5.   _____

6.   _____

7.   _____

8.   _____

Listen and write:

1.   _____

2.   _____

3.   _____

4.   _____

5.   _____

7.   _____

8.   _____

Initial Blends with **r**

Read the starting sounds: **ra re ri ro ru**

Read the blends and the words: Write the words twice:

bran   *bran*

1.	**b ra**	**bra**	**bran**
2.	**b re**	**bre**	**bred**
3.	b ri	bri	brim
4.	b ro	bro	broth
5.	b ru	bru	brush
6.	c ra	cra	crab
7.	c re	cre	credit
8.	c ri	cri	crib
9.	c ro	cro	crop
10.	c ru	cru	crush
11.	d ra	dra	drag
12.	d re	dre	dress
13.	d ri	dri	drip
14.	d ro	dro	drop
15.	d ru	dru	drug
16.	f ra	fra	Fran
17.	f re	fre	fresh
18.	f ri	fri	frill
19.	f ro	fro	frog
20.	f ru	fru	frump
21.			from*

From is a sight word. **o** = **ŭ** in **sun**.

Read the blends and the words: Write the words twice:

22. g ra   gra   grass   _____   _____

23. g re   gre   Greg   _____   _____

24. g ri   gri   grill   _____   _____

25. g ro   gro   grog   _____   _____

26. g ru   gru   gruff   _____   _____

27. p ra   pra   prance   _____   _____

28. p re   pre   press   _____   _____

29. p ri   pri   prim   _____   _____

30. p ro   pro   prom   _____   _____

31. t ra   tra   trap   _____   _____

32. t re   tre   trek   _____   _____

33. t ri   tri   trip   _____   _____

34. t ru   tru   trunk   _____   _____

Listen and write:

1. _____   8. _____   15. _____

2. _____   9. _____   16. _____

3. _____   10. _____   17. _____

4. _____   11. _____   18. _____

5. _____   12. _____   19. _____

6. _____   13. _____   20. _____

7. _____   14. _____   21. _____

More Initial Blends with **r**
(Including Special Endings: **ck**, **sh**, **ch**, **tch**, **th**, **wh**, **ce**, **ci**, **ge**, **gi**, **dge**)

Read the sounds and words:

1. b ra sh   brash
2. b ri ck   brick
3. b ri dge   bridge
4. b ro th   broth
5. c ra ck   crack
6. c ra sh   crash
7. c ro ck   crock
8. c ro tch   crotch
9. c ru sh   crush
10. d ru dge   drudge
11. f re sh   fresh
12. f ri dge   fridge
13. f ro th   froth
14. g ru dge   grudge
15. p ri ck   prick
16. t ra ck   track
17. t ra sh   trash
18. t ri ck   trick
19. t ro th   troth
20. t ru ck   truck
21. t ru dge   trudge

Write the words twice:

brash   *brash*

Listen and write:

1. _____

2. _____

3. _____

4. _____

5. _____

6. _____

7. _____

8. _____

9. _____

10. _____

11. _____

12. _____

13. _____

14. _____

15. _____

16. _____

17. _____

18. _____

19. _____

20. _____

21. _____

Sentences: Initial Blends with **r**

Read:

1. Fran will press the frill on her prom dress.
2. The fresh plums drop on the grass.
3. Do not drag that grill; it is hot!
4. Greg cannot crush the red brick.
5. A frog and a crab were in the brush.
6. Is that a brand of drug?
7. They trudge to the bridge and dredge the sludge.
8. The trip was fun! Give her credit for the plans.

Write:

1. _____

2. _____

3. _____

4. _____

5. _____

6. _____

7. _____
   _____

8. _____
   _____

Listen and write:

1. _____

2. _____

3. _____

4. _____

Other Initial Blends:
sc, sk, sm, sn, sp, st, sw, tw

Read the blends and the words: Write the words twice:

scab _____   *scab* _____

1.	s ca	sca	scab
2.	s ke	ske	sketch
3.	s ki	ski	skin
4.	s co	sco	Scott
5.	s cu	scu	scum
6.	s ma	sma	smack
7.	s me	sme	smell
8.	s mi	smi	Smith
9.	s mo	smo	smog
10.	s mu	smu	smug
11.	s na	sna	snack
12.	s ne	sne	snell
13.	s ni	sni	snip
14.	s no	sno	snob
15.	s nu	snu	snug
16.	s pa	spa	span
17.	s pe	spe	spell
18.	s pi	spi	spit
19.	s po	spo	spot
20.	s pu	spu	spud

Read the blends and the words: Write the words twice:

21. s ta   sta   stab   _____   _____

22. s te   ste   step   _____   _____

23. s ti   sti   stick   _____   _____

24. s to   sto   stop   _____   _____

25. s tu   stu   stuff   _____   _____

26. s wa   swa   swam   _____   _____

27. s wi   swi   switch   _____   _____

28. s wu   swu   swum   _____   _____

29. t wi   twi   twin   _____   _____

Listen and write:

1. _____   11. _____   21. _____

2. _____   12. _____   22. _____

3. _____   13. _____   23. _____

4. _____   14. _____   24. _____

5. _____   15. _____   25. _____

6. _____   16. _____   26. _____

7. _____   17. _____   27. _____

8. _____   18. _____   28. _____

9. _____   19. _____   29. _____

10. _____   20. _____   30. _____

Other Initial Blends
(Including Special Endings: **ck**, **sh**, **ch**, **tch**, **th**, **wh**, **ce**, **ci**, **ge**, **gi**, **dge**)

Read the sounds and words:

1.	s co tch	scotch
2.	s ma sh	smash
3.	s mo ck	smock
4.	s mu dge	smudge
5.	s na tch	snatch
6.	s ni tch	snitch
7.	s nu ck	snuck
8.	s pe ck	speck
9.	s ta ck	stack
10.	s ta sh	stash
11.	s ti ck	stick
12.	s ti tch	stitch
13.	s to ck	stock
14.	s tu ck	stuck
15.	s wi tch	switch
16.	t wi tch	twitch

Write the words twice:

scotch   *scotch*

_____   _____

_____   _____

_____   _____

_____   _____

_____   _____

_____   _____

_____   _____

_____   _____

_____   _____

_____   _____

_____   _____

_____   _____

_____   _____

_____   _____

_____   _____

Listen and write:

1. _____	8. _____	15. _____
2. _____	9. _____	16. _____
3. _____	10. _____	17. _____
4. _____	11. _____	18. _____
5. _____	12. _____	19. _____
6. _____	13. _____	20. _____
7. _____	14. _____	21. _____

Sentences: Other Initial Blends

Read:

1. Miss Smith can swim, sketch, and stitch.
2. Scott has a scab on his skin.
3. The smog and scum smell bad!
4. The snobs at that club will snub them.
5. Stash the sticks on the steps.
6. If the rat sniffs the snack, it will snatch it up!
7. I am stuck and cannot spell today. Can we switch to math?
8. This smock has spots, smudges, rips, and specks.

Write:

1. _____
2. _____
3. _____
4. _____
5. _____
6. _____

   _____
7. _____

   _____
8. _____

Listen and write:

1. _____
2. _____
3. _____
4. _____

Special Skill

PREVIEWING WORDS OF THREE OR MORE SYLLABLES
FROM THE STORY The Drop-In Clinic

Remember that each syllable has one vowel sound.

Read syllables:	Read words:	Write the words:
1. ben e fit	benefit	_____
2. blem ish es	blemishes	_____
3. cin na mon	cinnamon	_____
4. ep i dem ic	epidemic	_____
5. gel a tin	gelatin	_____
6. reg i men	regimen	_____

Listen and write:

1. _____   4. _____

2. _____   5. _____

3. _____   6. _____

Story 5

Read: **The Drop-In Clinic**

Are you sick? Do you have a problem? If you do, you can go to the Drop-In   **1**
Clinic. The Drop-In Clinic is for the public's benefit. It is for men, women, and
children. It is the red brick clinic on the block with the bridge. You can get to it in a
truck, bus, or cab. The staff has skills to get you well. On the clinic staff are Dr.
Winston Blum, Dr. Chun Chen, Dr. Brad Clifton, Dr. Gretchen Pratt, Dr. Fran
Pressman, Dr. Be Van Tran, and Dr. Bridget Twitchell. They have no slick tricks.
They pledge to give you a plan to get you well.

You can come to the Drop-In Clinic when you want to. You can "drop in." You   **2**
do not have to plan in advance. Punch in at the clock, and the staff will come and
fetch you. You do not have to have cash, since they have a credit plan. You can give
them a check, too.

Do you or the children have to have checkups or shots? Did you get sick in an   **3**
epidemic? If so, come to the Drop-In Clinic.

Do you have a rash, a blotch, or a blemish? Do you blush or flush too much? **4**
Do you have spots or specks? If you do, Dr. Be Van Tran has a plan for you. If you do
his skin regimen, you can get rid of some of the rashes, blotches, or blemishes in a
flash.

Did you get a cut, a stab, or a slash (such as from glass)? If the flesh is slit and **5**
it has bled, then come to the Drop-In Clinic today. Dr. Fran Pressman will blot and
stitch the flap of skin. When a scab comes, the stitches will go and you will be well.

Do you want to get fit and trim? Do you want to get rid of flab? If you do, the **6**
Drop-In Clinic has a fitness regimen, which Dr. Chun Chen and Dr. Bridget Twitchell
run.

In this plan you can swim and jog on the track, within limits which Dr. Chen **7**
will set for you. You can switch if you want to. If you swim, you can switch to track,
but you do have to do something to get slim. You cannot do nothing. You cannot bluff
Dr. Chen.

Dr. Twitchell tells you what stuff you can have, what to stock up on, and what **8**
to give up. You can stock the fridge with things such as fresh plums, lettuce, bran,
gelatin, and a crock full of broth (if you skin off the fat). You can grill flatfish, frogs'
legs, clams, and crabs. Then you can crush lemon and cinnamon sticks, and put them
on top. You cannot be a glutton on this plan. You will have to limit snacks. You
cannot have flapjacks, flan, fudge, or giblets. You cannot slack off. Stick with it. The
plan is not blissful, but you will benefit from it. You will thank and bless the clinic
staff when you are fit and trim.

Did you jog on the track and trip? Did you slip on a step or slick grass? If you **9**
said "yes," Dr. Brad Clifton will be glad to check you. He can set a crack in a rib and
set legs, too. To get well, he will tell you to flex and stretch.

Do you box in a club? Did you get black and blue? If you did, drop in to the **10**
clinic and the staff will patch you up. You can tell them that you box for fun (you did
not have a grudge). You were in a match yesterday. You got some punches, slugs,
slaps, and smacks. The staff will then tell you not to box until you are well.

Do you have a problem with drugs, such as crack? Do you have a drug habit?   **11**
Do you want to stop? If you do, the Drop-In Clinic has a plan to get you off drugs. You
can live well with no drugs. The staff will put you on this track.

Do you have lots of bad days? Are you glum? Do problems stack up so much   **12**
that you think they will crush you? Do you have spells when you are blue? Do you
think you are a drudge? Did the boss let you go? Do you skip class? Do you drag and
plop into bed? Are you stuck in a rut? If yes, come to the Drop-In Clinic. Discuss
things with Dr. Winston Blum. He will not grill you or press you or give you a lot of
flack. He is not smug or brash or gruff. You can blab as much as you want. Tell him
the problem you have, but do not be glib. With Dr. Blum, you can dispel lots of
problems.

If you want a checkup or a fitness plan, or you are sick or have problems, you   **13**
can benefit a lot from the Drop-In Clinic.

Story 5 emphasizes:
- initial blends with **l** and **r**
- other initial blends with **s, c, k, m, n, p, t, w**

and includes selections from:
- two-syllable, short-vowel words and names
- verb + **s** (third-person singular); noun + **'s** (possessive)
- special sounds: **ck, sh, ch, tch, th, wh, ce, ci, ge, gi, dge**
- sight words: **for, or, want, too, women, today, yesterday, was, were, thing, nothing, something, think, thank, what, from**
- three- and four-syllable words: **benefit, blemishes, cinnamon, epidemic, gelatin, regimen**

Introduction to Final Blends

Final blends are two or more consonants at the end of a word. They are made by running the sounds of the two consonants together. Each consonant keeps its own sound; they just come close together. For example:

Read each word, then add one
more sound at the end of the word: Write the words twice:

1. ram   ram p   ramp   *ramp*   *ramp*

2. pan   pan t   pant   _____   _____

3. fun   fun d   fund   _____   _____

FINAL BLENDS

Read these final blends with the vowels that come before them. Then read and write the words with the blends.

Read: Write:

1. **ct**   ac **t**:   act   _____   _____

                            fact   _____   _____

                            tact   _____   _____

              ec **t**:   sect   _____   _____

              uc **t**:   duct   _____   _____

2. **ft**   af **t**:   aft   _____   _____

              ef **t**:   left   _____   _____

              if **t**:   gift   _____   _____

                            lift   _____   _____

                            rift   _____   _____

                            sift   _____   _____

                            swift   _____   _____

              of **t**:   loft   _____   _____

                            soft   _____   _____

Read: Write:

3. **ld**   **el d**:   he**ld**

        meld

        weld

4. **lf**   **el f**:   e**lf**

        self

    ol f: go**lf**

    ul f: gu**lf**

5. **lk**   **el k**:   e**lk**

        Welk

    il k: i**lk**

        bilk

        milk

        silk

    ul k: bu**lk**

        hulk

        sulk

6. **lm**   **el m**:   e**lm**

        helm

7. **lp**   **el p**:   he**lp**

        kelp

        whelp

    ul p: gu**lp**

        pulp

8. **lt**   **el t**:   be**lt**

        felt

        melt

        pelt

        welt

Read: Write:

           il t: ki**lt**   _____   _____

                    lilt   _____   _____

                    silt   _____   _____

                    tilt   _____   _____

                    wilt   _____   _____

           ul t: adu**lt**   _____   _____

9. **mp** am p: a**mp**   _____   _____

                    camp   _____   _____

                    damp   _____   _____

                    lamp   _____   _____

                    ramp   _____   _____

                    tamp   _____   _____

                    vamp   _____   _____

           em p: he**mp**   _____   _____

                    Kemp   _____   _____

10. **mp** im p: i**mp**   _____   _____

                    gimp   _____   _____

                    limp   _____   _____

                    wimp   _____   _____

           om p: po**mp**   _____   _____

                    romp   _____   _____

           um p: bu**mp**   _____   _____

                    dump   _____   _____

                    hump   _____   _____

                    jump   _____   _____

                    lump   _____   _____

                    pump   _____   _____

                    rump   _____   _____

                    sump   _____   _____

Read: Write:

11. **nd**   **an d**:   **and**   _____   _____

                            band   _____   _____

                            hand   _____   _____

                            land   _____   _____

                            Rand   _____   _____

                            sand   _____   _____

12. **nd**   **en d**:   **end**   _____   _____

                            bend   _____   _____

                            fend   _____   _____

                            lend   _____   _____

                            mend   _____   _____

                            pend   _____   _____

                            rend   _____   _____

                            send   _____   _____

                            tend   _____   _____

                            vend   _____   _____

                            wend   _____   _____

               in d: **Lind**   _____   _____

                            wind   _____   _____

               on d: **bond**   _____   _____

                            fond   _____   _____

                            pond   _____   _____

               un d: **fund**   _____   _____

                            Lund   _____   _____

Read: Write:

13. **nt**   **an t:**   **ant**   _____   _____

                             can't*   _____   _____

                             pant   _____   _____

                             rant   _____   _____

                             infant   _____   _____

14. **nt**   **en t:**   **bent**   _____   _____

                             dent   _____   _____

                             lent   _____   _____

                             pent   _____   _____

                             rent   _____   _____

                             sent   _____   _____

                             tent   _____   _____

                             vent   _____   _____

                             went   _____   _____

                             indent   _____   _____

          in t: **dint**   _____   _____

                             hint   _____   _____

                             lint   _____   _____

                             mint   _____   _____

                             tint   _____   _____

          un t: **bunt**   _____   _____

                             hunt   _____   _____

                             Lunt   _____   _____

                             punt   _____   _____

                             runt   _____   _____

*__Can't__ is the contraction of **cannot.** See page 212.

Read: Write:

15. **pt**   ap **t**:   a**pt**   _____   _____

                            r**apt**   _____   _____

                 e**p t**:   ke**pt**   _____   _____

                            we**pt**   _____   _____

16. **sk**   a**s k**:   a**sk**   _____   _____

                            b**ask**   _____   _____

                            c**ask**   _____   _____

                            m**ask**   _____   _____

                            t**ask**   _____   _____

                e**s k**:   de**sk**   _____   _____

                i**s k**:   Fi**sk**   _____   _____

                            whi**sk**   _____   _____

                u**s k**:   du**sk**   _____   _____

                            hu**sk**   _____   _____

                            mu**sk**   _____   _____

                            Ru**sk**   _____   _____

                            tu**sk**   _____   _____

17. **st**   a**s t**:   ca**st**   _____   _____

                            fa**st**   _____   _____

                            la**st**   _____   _____

                            ma**st**   _____   _____

                            pa**st**   _____   _____

                            va**st**   _____   _____

Read: Write:

es t: best   _____   _____

           nest   _____   _____

           pest   _____   _____

           test   _____   _____

           vest   _____   _____

           west   _____   _____

           zest   _____   _____

18. st   is t: fist   _____   _____

           gist   _____   _____

           list   _____   _____

           mist   _____   _____

     us t: bust   _____   _____

           dust   _____   _____

           gust   _____   _____

           lust   _____   _____

           must   _____   _____

           rust   _____   _____

19. sp   as p: asp   _____   _____

           gasp   _____   _____

           hasp   _____   _____

           rasp   _____   _____

     is p: lisp   _____   _____

           wisp   _____   _____

     us p: cusp   _____   _____

Listen and write:

1. _____   4. _____   7. _____

2. _____   5. _____   8. _____

3. _____   6. _____   9. _____

Sentences: Final Blends

Read:

1.   The adults will fund the kids' band at the camp.

2.   Did Ms. Rand put the hemp belt on the silk pants herself?

3.   Quick! Dump the kelp with the ants on the damp sand.

4.   Dr. Welk held a pump in her left hand.

5.   West of that vast land mass are the last of the elk.

6.   The wind on his back will help him jump into the pond.

7.   I felt mad when he kept the rent, cash, and bonds!

8.   Mr. Kemp must do the rest of the tasks himself.

Write:

1.   *The adults will fund the kids' band at the camp.*

2.   _____

_____

3.   _____

_____

4.   _____

_____

5.   _____

_____

6.   _____

_____

7.   _____

_____

8.   _____

Listen and write:

1. _____

_____

2. _____

_____

3. _____

_____

4. _____

_____

5. _____

_____

6. _____

_____

7. _____

_____

8. _____

_____

9. _____

_____

10. _____

_____

11. _____

_____

12. _____

_____

Special Skill

**PREVIEWING WORDS OF THREE OR MORE SYLLABLES
FROM THE STORY Camp West Wind**

Remember that each syllable has one vowel sound.

Read syllables:	Read words:	Write the words:
1. cat a ma ran	catamaran	_____
2. con tes tant	contestant	_____
3. e lev en	eleven	_____
4. ep i log	epilog	_____
5. hab i tat	habitat	_____
6. jav e lin	javelin	_____

Listen and write:

1. _____   4. _____

2. _____   5. _____

3. _____   6. _____

Story 6

Camp
West Wind

Read: **Camp West Wind**

Camp West Wind is in Tampa, Florida. It is on a vast tract of land with a   **1**
pond. Fresh brisk winds drift in from the Gulf, which is west of the camp. The camp is
for adults and children. Moms and dads can attend with the children. A kid will still
do a lot of things and have to fend for himself or herself. The adults and children live
in cabins that have lofts but no lamps. On trips from the camp, they have slept in
tents.

The camp has lots of things to do, such as crafts, golf, tennis, and track. For   **2**
track, you can toss the javelin and the discus, or you can run and jump. You can swim
in the Gulf, too. If you want, you can attempt to pass a swim test, which is held at the
end of camp. In the test, you have to swim from the sand to the bridge and back. If
you want to do nothing and just rest on the sand, you can bask in the sun (but not until
you "melt"). You can sift the soft sand, tamp the damp sand, and collect kelp. You
can hunt for mollusk shells, such as whelks, chestnut mussels, conches, clams, and
scallops.

For a project, you can construct a raft or a catamaran. A contest is held at the   **3**
end of camp, and you can be a contestant. Judges will tell which raft or catamaran is
the swiftest. It is fun to construct, but it is a big task. The raft or catamaran must
have a mast. It must have a helm aft of the mast, too. You must have a vest on when
you are on the craft, since a gust of wind can tilt it. Are you the fastest? Are you the
best? Are you second? Or are you last? The swiftest raft or catamaran wins the
contest.

You can ask to fish for shrimp in the Gulf, but you cannot catch cusk in Florida   **4**
since it is too hot. You cannot hunt at Camp West Wind, and you must not have a

handgun. You cannot kill or get pelts or tusks at this camp. It is a habitat for muskrats, ducks, and frogs, which swim in the pond. Robins' nests are in the elms. Insects buzz, and ants dig big anthills. At dusk, a mist is on the pond, and you can smell a hint of musk.

Since the men, women, and children have so much to do at Camp West Wind, **5** Mrs. Clift of the camp staff tends to the infants. She is fond of infants and gives them milk, lunch, snacks, and lots of rest.

At dusk, the adults and children go to the Lodge. Some sit on rattan benches. **6** Some kids jump and romp. The children have a band, "The Clefs," with eleven drums and twelve trumpets. It uplifts them. Some of the children act. Some of them have masks on. In the cast are a prince and a princess, a dragon, and an elf (the elf is the culprit). The cast acts to the hilt: The prince comes in, with a lot of pomp, to a blast of the trumpets. He sits on the rump of an elf. The dragon—a big hulk that sulks—pants and tramps in. The cast rants and yells with zest. The elf clutches the princess, but she is swift and punches the culprit. The prince clasps the princess's left hand and drags her from the elf. The dragon attempts to stop them, but they have fled. Elfin culprits and dragons that sulk cannot entrap them! In the end, the princess and prince win. The women, men, and children gulp and grasp on to the benches. They were rapt. When the prince and princess were in a trap, some felt sad and wistful and kept still. Some of the children wept. Did they clap at the end? You bet they did!

Epilog

Mr. and Mrs. Lund went to Camp West Wind when they were children. They **7** had lots of fun at the camp, so they have given a fund that has kept it up. What a gift! The days are full at Camp West Wind. Adults and children of today think of what the Lunds did for them "yesterday." They are thankful to them.

Story 6 emphasizes:
- final blends: **ct, ft, ld, lf, lk, lm, lp, lt, mp, nd, nt, pt, sk, sp, st**

and includes selections from:
- two-syllable, short-vowel words and names
- verb + **s** (third-person singular); noun + **'s** (possessive)
- special sounds: **ck, sh, ch, tch, th, wh, ce, ci, ge, gi, dge**
- initial blends with **l, r, s, c, k, m, n, p, t, w**
- sight words: **for, or, want, too, women, today, yesterday, was, were, thing, nothing, something, think, thank, what, from**
- three- and four-syllable words: **catamaran, contestant, eleven, epilog, habitat, javelin**

Review: Initial and Final Blends

The following words have both initial and final blends. Underline the blends in the Read column and write the words in the Write column.

Read:	Write:		Read:	Write:
1. **bland**	*bland*		23. crisp	_____
2. blast	_____		24. crump	_____
3. blend	_____		25. crust	_____
4. blimp	_____		26. draft	_____
5. blond	_____		27. drift	_____
6. blunt	_____		28. flask	_____
7. bract	_____		29. flint	_____
8. brand	_____		30. frisk	_____
9. Brent	_____		31. frump	_____
10. brisk	_____		32. gland	_____
11. brunt	_____		33. glimpse	_____
12. clamp	_____		34. glint	_____
13. clasp	_____		35. graft	_____
14. cleft	_____		36. grand	_____
15. Clint	_____		37. grant	_____
16. clomp	_____		38. grasp	_____
17. clump	_____		39. grist	_____
18. craft	_____		40. grump	_____
19. cramp	_____		41. grunt	_____
20. crept	_____		42. plant	_____
21. crest	_____		43. plump	_____
22. crimp	_____		44. primp	_____

Read: Write: Read: Write:

45. **print** _____   57. stamp _____

46. quest _____   58. stand _____

47. scalp _____   59. stint _____

48. scamp _____   60. stomp _____

49. scant _____   61. stump _____

50. skimp _____   62. stunt _____

51. slant _____   63. swift _____

52. slept _____   64. tramp _____

53. slump _____   65. trump _____

54. slunk _____   66. trust _____

55. smelt _____   67. twist _____

56. spent _____   68. front* _____

Listen and write:

1. _____   11. _____   21. _____

2. _____   12. _____   22. _____

3. _____   13. _____   23. _____

4. _____   14. _____   24. _____

5. _____   15. _____   25. _____

6. _____   16. _____   26. _____

7. _____   17. _____   27. _____

8. _____   18. _____   28. _____

9. _____   19. _____   29. _____

10. _____   20. _____   30. _____

***Front** is a sight word. In this word, **o** = ŭ, so it sounds like **sun**.

Review: Two-Syllable Words with Initial and Final Blends and the Special Sounds
ck, sh, ch, tch, th, wh, ce, ci, ge, gi, dge

Read the syllables and words: Write: Listen and write:

1. Bra zil   Brazil   *Brazil* _____   _____
2. con duct   conduct   _____   _____
3. con flict   conflict   _____   _____
4. con tract   contract   _____   _____
5. den tist   dentist   _____   _____
6. em blem   emblem   _____   _____
7. ex press   express   _____   _____
8. ex tract   extract   _____   _____
9. fresh man   freshman   _____   _____
10. gad get   gadget   _____   _____
11. im press   impress   _____   _____
12. in ject   inject   _____   _____
13. in sult   insult   _____   _____
14. judg ment   judgment   _____   _____
15. ob ject   object   _____   _____
16. preg nant   pregnant   _____   _____
17. prod uct   product   _____   _____
18. prog ress   progress   _____   _____
19. proj ect   project   _____   _____
20. sec ond   second   _____   _____
21. sub ject   subject   _____   _____
22. trans gress   transgress   _____   _____
23. trans mit   transmit   _____   _____
24. trans plant   transplant   _____   _____
25. Pat rick   Patrick   _____   _____

Review: Sentences Using Words with Initial and Final Blends

Read:

1. Since Patrick sent the contract express, we can do the project.
2. The sand drifts on the swift, brisk wind.
3. Extract that clump of plants and then transplant them.
4. Clint is plump, blond, and has a cleft in his chin.
5. Print the draft, stamp it, and send it to Brenda.
6. If you trust him, stand with him, and do not have a conflict.
7. The muffin was bland but had a crisp crust.
8. That dentist is blunt and is a grump!

Write:

1. _____

    _____

2. _____

    _____

3. _____

    _____

4. _____

    _____

5. _____

    _____

6. _____

    _____

7. _____

    _____

8. _____

    _____

Listen and write:

1. _____

_____

2. _____

_____

3. _____

_____

4. _____

_____

5. _____

_____

6. _____

_____

7. _____

_____

8. _____

_____

9. _____

_____

10. _____

_____

11. _____

_____

12. _____

_____

Special Skill:

PREVIEWING WORDS OF THREE OR MORE SYLLABLES
FROM THE STORY Trent's Dress and Pants Shop

Remember that each syllable has one vowel sound.

Read syllables:	Read words:	Write the words:
1. ban dan nas	bandannas	_____
2. cat a log	catalog	_____
3. el e gant	elegant	_____
4. ex cel lent	excellent	_____
5. moc ca sins	moccasins	_____
6. Pan a ma	Panama	_____
7. Pris cil la	Priscilla	_____
8. taf fe ta	taffeta	_____

Listen and write:

1. _____   5. _____

2. _____   6. _____

3. _____   7. _____

4. _____   8. _____

Story 7

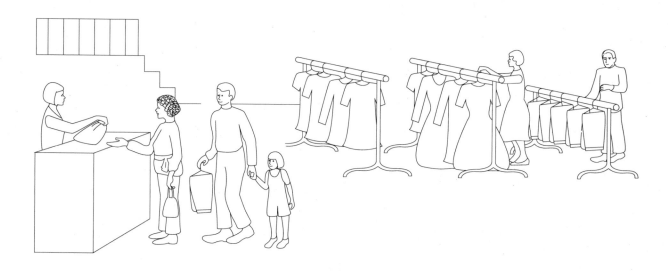

Read: **Trent's Dress and Pants Shop**

The Catalog

Trent's Dress and Pants Shop has hundreds of dresses and pants to sell. The shop is   **1**
vast, and you can get the best trends and brands. If you cannot come in, Trent's will
send you what you want. You can shop with the catalog. Trent's has things for adults
(women and men) as well as for infants and children. You can get elegant dresses for
proms, swim trunks for camp, golf pants for the club, and things of that ilk. At
Trent's, you can "dress for success" on the job or get denim pants to go to a ranch in
the West.

If you want pants or a dress to be bland or have a lot of jazz, come to Trent's. If   **2**
you want to be prim or a vamp, if you are slim or plump, you can get something just for
you at Trent's.

If you have a big budget or you have to scrimp on what you spend, Trent's has   **3**
something for you. You can get gifts at Trent's, too.

Fabrics

Some of the fabrics and cloth come from Brazil, Finland, Scotland, and France. The   **4**
fabrics and cloth in stock are silk, cotton, linen, muslin, denim, velvet, felt, hemp,
satin, flannel, canvas, chintz, duck, duffel, net, poplin, taffeta, twill, and damask.

Prom Dresses

Prom dresses come with frills and ribbons. Some come with straps or are strapless.   **5**
Some are backless. Some are cut full or with a slit so you can get a glimpse of leg.
You can select from:

- plush black velvet dresses with glass buttons in back and handbags with a brass clasp to match
- soft silk dresses in a plum tint with a pink frill at the hem and neck and a wisp of pink net on top of the silk
- velvet dresses in a sand tint with a hint of rust in the stitches at the hem. They snap up the back.

Classic Day Dresses

Day dresses come in prints and solids. You can select from: **6**

- crisp linen dresses in mint with green clutch bags and felt hats. On the brims of the hats are yellow buds.
- milk-white cotton dresses with slips that match and tan hemp belts. They come with a brass pin that clips on at the neck.
- jacket dresses in a cotton-linen blend with a print of black flecks on mist blue and a black patent belt. For buttons, the jackets have frogs put on with hand stitches.

Extra Things

You can select from: **7**

- chintz smocks with prints for pregnant women
- Scottish kilts (You can pick the clan you want.)
- pants (some have vests to match; some have studs to dress them up):
     —blue denim   —gray flannel slacks
     —white ducks   —twill britches
- flats, pumps, clogs, flip-flops, sandals, and moccasins
- socks, chaps, ascots, bandannas, cravats, and neckbands
- Panama or Stetson hats

The Loft

In the loft of Trent's, men and women sit and stitch the dresses and pants. They sit on   **8**
benches at desks. The smell of cloth fills the loft. Lots of steps go into a dress:

Step 1: Tran drafts sketches of the dresses. The boss will glimpse the sketches and tell Tran what she wants. Then Tran will do a second draft.

Step 2: Frances cuts the dresses. She snips the cloth, picks up the bits, and drops them into the trash. Then she puts the cut dresses in a stack on a shelf.

Step 3: Patrick pins the cut dresses. He has his glasses on. It is a trick not to stick himself with the pins. Then he stacks the dresses.

Step 4: Kristen stitches the dresses.

Step 5: Clint hems the bottoms with hand stitches. He can stitch with the hemstitch, backstitch, whipstitch, tent stitch, slip stitch, and twist stitch.

Step 6: Brenda brushes the lint off the dresses, presses them, blocks them, and puts them in plastic bags. Then she packs them flat in boxes so as not to crush them. The boxes are full to the brim.

Step 7: Brad slaps tags on the boxes. Then he stamps the boxes with the shop's brand, **TRENT'S**.

Step 8: Greg drags the boxes to the truck, lifts them in, and stacks them. He will ship them from this dock.

A Problem in the Loft

A problem at this shop is the boss on the second shift. He is an ill-bred, tactless clod. **9** He is gruff, brash, and smug with the help. He stomps and clomps into the loft. He has crept up on the men and women as they stitch, too! He is too strict. He will not let you get up if you have cramps, are stiff, or have to stretch or rest. Gretchen and Stan get the brunt of his ill will. The boss will not let them stop to have a snack. When he spots them at rest, he has said, "Is this a stunt? You are slothful! Do not slack off!"

Gretchen and Stan have a lot of pluck. They have spunk and are blunt with **10** him. They tell the boss, "We do the best job we can. Do not bug us or we will picket this shop!"

Models

To help sell the stock, Trent's has models. **11**

Today is a big event. A tent is set up for the models. On this day, Priscilla **12** models. She has to primp and put on "blush." Priscilla comes in clad in a trim jacket dress. She flits and prances across the ramp and is grand.

She will not slump or flush. She can stand and not twitch. Priscilla will not **13** flub it. She has spent the day—a big stint—as a model. She has not slept and will crash at the end of the day and flop into bed.

The Custom Shop

If you want to adjust something that you get at the shop, Bridget and Clem will do it **14**
for you. They have a lot of talent and are excellent at this craft! They will fit the
crotch of the pants or give an uplift to the bust. They can expand the span across the
chest or extend the cuffs. They can tuck in the back and give you a snug fit. They can
mend a rip in a cuff or put a vent in a jacket. They can add a clasp, stitch a crest on a
pocket, and add a clump of buds to the brim of a hat.

Come to Trent's Today!

Do you want something? Come to Trent's! You will be glad you did. It has pants, **15**
dresses, smocks, and lots of extra things to go with them. They have gifts for you to
give, too. Trent's has what you want, when you want it!

Story 7 emphasizes:
* initial and final blends

and includes selections from:
* two-syllable, short-vowel words and names
* verb + **s** (third-person singular); noun + **'s** (possessive)
* special sounds: **ck, sh, ch, tch, th, wh, ce, ci, ge, gi, dge**
* sight words: **for, or, want, too, women, today, yesterday, was, were, thing, nothing, think, thank, what, from**
* three- and four-syllable words and names: **bandannas, catalog, elegant, excellent, moccasins, Panama, Priscilla, taffeta**

Bonus Page: Short-Vowel Words with Three or More Syllables Including Blends and Special Sounds

Remember that each syllable has one vowel sound.

Read syllables:	Read words:	Write the words:
1. bot a nist	botanist	_____
2. Breck en ridge	Breckenridge	_____
3. com pe tence	competence	_____
4. con fi dence	confidence	_____
5. de scen dant	descendant	_____
6. dil i gence	diligence	_____
7. dra ma tist	dramatist	_____
8. ec stat ic	ecstatic	_____
9. ex cel lent	excellent	_____
10. ex plic it	explicit	_____
11. ful fill ment	fulfillment	_____
12. im mi grant	immigrant	_____
13. im ple ment	implement	_____
14. in trin sic	intrinsic	_____
15. list less ness	listlessness	_____
16. mil i tant	militant	_____
17. nov el ist	novelist	_____
18. plac id ness	placidness	_____
19. prom i nent	prominent	_____
20. skel e ton	skeleton	_____
21. skill ful ness	skillfulness	_____
22. as ton ish ment	astonishment	_____

Listen and write:

1. _____
2. _____
3. _____
4. _____
5. _____
6. _____
7. _____
8. _____
9. _____
10. _____
11. _____
12. _____
13. _____
14. _____
15. _____
16. _____
17. _____
18. _____
19. _____
20. _____
21. _____
22. _____
23. _____
24. _____
25. _____

26. _____
27. _____
28. _____
29. _____
30. _____
31. _____
32. _____
33. _____
34. _____
35. _____
36. _____
37. _____
38. _____
39. _____
40. _____
41. _____
42. _____
43. _____
44. _____
45. _____
46. _____
47. _____
48. _____
49. _____
50. _____

Bonus Page: Sentences Using Short-Vowel Words with Three or More Syllables Including Blends and Special Sounds

Read:

1. Mr. Breckenridge is a novelist. His novels are full of explicit sentences.
2. As a botanist, Dr. Grant is excellent with plants.
3. Mrs. Brickman, a prominent dramatist, still lacks confidence in herself.
4. Is he a descendant of immigrants from France and Scotland?
5. The staff's astonishment at Mr. Frost's diligence was an insult.
6. Greg's competence is intrinsic to his skillfulness at golf.
7. Fran was ecstatic at her test results on the frog's skeleton.

Write:

1. _____

_____

2. _____

_____

3. _____

_____

4. _____

_____

5. _____

_____

6. _____

_____

7. _____

_____

Bonus Page: Pronouncing Words with Three-Consonant Blends

For help in pronunciation, these words have been broken into parts (not syllables).

Pronounce:	Read:	Write:
1. sp ri g	sprig	_____
2. sp ri nt	sprint	_____
3. st ri p	strip	_____
4. st ra nd	strand	_____
5. st ra p	strap	_____
6. st ru m	strum	_____
7. in st ru ct	instruct	_____
8. con st ri ct	constrict	_____
9. fif th	fifth	_____
10. six th	sixth	_____
11. ten th	tenth	_____
12. sev en th	seventh	_____

Listen and write:

1. _____   7. _____

2. _____   8. _____

3. _____   9. _____

4. _____   10. _____

5. _____   11. _____

6. _____   12. _____

CHAPTER 5:
Other Word Endings

In this chapter, you will read, write, compare, and review other word endings including

- **le** (as in bubb**le**)
- **al** (as in dent**al**)
- **y** (as in happ**y**)
- **ly** (as in sad**ly**)
- **ing** (as in k**ing**)
- **ang** (as in b**ang**)
- **ong** (as in s**ong**)
- **ung** (as in s**ung**)
- **eng** (as in l**eng**th)

- **ink** (as in w**ink**)
- **ank** (as in b**ank**)
- **onk** (as in h**onk**)
- **unk** (as in d**unk**)
- **enk** (as in J**enk**ins)
- **ed** = **id** (as in land**ed**)
- **ed** = **d** (as in fill**ed**)
- **ed** = **t** (as in jump**ed**)
- **er** (as in runn**er**, bigg**er**)

You also will learn two special skills in forming **ing** words:

1. when to double consonants before **ing** (pat—pat**ting**)
2. when to drop the **e** before **ing** (gigg**le**—gigg**ling**)

and two special skills in forming **ed** words:

3. when **y** changes to **i** before **ed** (stud**y**—stud**ied**)
4. when to double the consonant before **ed** (pat—pat**ted**)

You will learn one special skill in forming **er** words:

5. when to double consonants before **er** (run—run**ner**)

In addition, you will read, write, and review sentences and stories that emphasize these lessons and contain words with three or more syllables.

Sound: le

candle

The **le** sound sounds like the end of the word **pull**.

Read: le   le   le   le   le   le   le   le   le   le   le   le   le

Write: _____

Listen and
write: _____

COMPARE

Read: le   pull   full   ble   dle   gle   ple   tle   le   ble   dle   gle

        ple   tle   le   ble   dle   gle   ple   tle   le   ble   dle   gle   ple

Write: _____

_____

Listen and
write: _____

_____

WORDS

Read syllables:		Write syllables:	Read words:	Write words twice:
1.	can	**dle**	can dle	candle	*candle* *candle*
2.	bub	**ble**	_____ _____	bubble	_____ _____
3.	mid	**dle**	_____ _____	middle	_____ _____
4.	wig	**gle**	_____ _____	wiggle	_____ _____
5.	lit	**tle**	_____ _____	little	_____ _____
6.	ap	**ple**	_____ _____	apple	_____ _____

Listen and write:

1. _____   4. _____   7. _____   10. _____

2. _____   5. _____   8. _____   11. _____

3. _____   6. _____   9. _____   12. _____

Sentences Using Words with the **le** Ending

Additional words with the **le** ending:

babble	middle	haggle	sickle	gentle	fizzle
dribble	fiddle	waggle	tickle	battle	drizzle
nibble	coddle	giggle	buckle	cattle	frizzle
wobble	cuddle	jiggle	chuckle	rattle	sizzle
bubble	muddle	wiggle	ample	tattle	guzzle
rubble	puddle	smuggle	sample	kettle	muzzle
gamble	candle	snuggle	trample	mettle	nuzzle
ramble	handle	boggle	temple	settle	puzzle
bramble	kindle	goggle	dimple	brittle	razzle-dazzle
nimble	fondle	freckle	simple	bottle	
thimble	bundle	speckle	apple	dazzle	
meddle	trundle	fickle	dapple	frazzle	
peddle	gaggle	pickle	grapple	nozzle	

Read:

1. In the bramble, rabbits nibble on the ample carrots.
2. Do little kids with dimples and freckles giggle a lot?
3. If he tickles his gentle dog, it will wiggle and nuzzle him.
4. He is nimble and can handle a thimble well.
5. When it drizzles, she bundles up and tramples in the puddles.
6. In the middle of the battle, he fell on the rubble.

Write:

1. _____
2. _____
3. _____
4. _____
5. _____
6. _____

Listen and write:

1. _____
2. _____
3. _____

Sound: al

signal

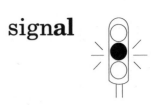

This sound also sounds like the end of the word **pull**.

Read: al   al   al   al   al   al   al   al   al   al   al   al

Write: _____

Listen and
write: _____

COMPARE

Read: al   pull   full   al   el   dle   ple   mal   cal   nal   tal

            al   pull   full   al   el   dle   ple   mal   cal   nal   tal

Write: _____

_____

Listen and
write: _____

_____

WORDS

Read syllables: Write syllables: Read words: Write words twice:

1. sig **nal** <u>sig</u> <u>nal</u> sig**nal** *signal* *signal*

2. den **tal** _____ _____ den**tal** _____ _____

3. cen **tral** _____ _____ cen**tral** _____ _____

4. an i **mal** _____ ___ _____ ani**mal** _____ _____

5. hos pi **tal** _____ ___ _____ hospi**tal** _____ _____

6. med i **cal** _____ ___ _____ medi**cal** _____ _____

Listen and write:

1. _____   4. _____   7. _____   10. _____

2. _____   5. _____   8. _____   11. _____

3. _____   6. _____   9. _____   12. _____

Sentences Using Words with the **al** Ending

Additional words with the **al** ending:

pe**dal**	ven**tral**	skele**tal**
me**tal**	capi**tal**	pivo**tal**
pe**tal**	comi**cal**	tacti**cal**
dis**mal**	pedes**tal**	festi**val**
fis**cal**	classi**cal**	sentimen**tal**
scan**dal**	princi**pal**	

Read:

1. Did you go to the dental and medical clinics yesterday?
2. Pedal to the signal since it is in a central spot.
3. On the bottom of the fish is a ventral fin.
4. The vet at the animal hospital is a comical man!
5. Can you dance to classical and rock?
6. In that fiscal scandal they lost capital and principal.

Write:

1. _____
   _____
2. _____
3. _____
4. _____
   _____
5. _____
6. _____
   _____

Listen and write:

1. _____
2. _____
3. _____

Sound: y

happy

The **y** sound sounds like the **e** in **he**.

Read: y y y y y y y y y y y y y y y

Write: _____

Listen and
write: _____

COMPARE

Read: y he y me y she y be y we pull le y full le y

       y he y me y she y be y we pull le y full le y

Write: _____

_____

Listen and
write: _____

_____

WORDS

Read syllables:		Write syllables:		Read words:	Write words twice:	
1.	hap	py	hap	py	happy	*happy* *happy*
2.	fun	ny	___	___	funny	___ ___
3.	sun	ny	___	___	sunny	___ ___
4.	fog	gy	___	___	foggy	___ ___
5.	lob	by	___	___	lobby	___ ___
6.	han	dy	___	___	handy	___ ___

Listen and write:

1. _____   4. _____   7. _____   10. _____

2. _____   5. _____   8. _____   11. _____

3. _____   6. _____   9. _____   12. _____

Sentences Using Words with the y Ending

Additional words with the **y** ending:

Bobby	Peggy	bunny	puppy	Perry	musty
hobby	groggy	gunny	berry	Terry	rusty
snobby	itchy	runny	ferry	Sherry	crusty
muddy	filthy	nippy	cherry	city	Patty
candy	dummy	zippy	Jerry	shanty	kitty
dandy	mummy	copy	Kerry	plenty	witty
sandy	crummy	poppy	merry	twenty	fuddy-duddy
body	yummy	guppy	very	dusty	gunnysack

Read:

1. Terry said that her bunny and puppy are funny.

2. The trip to the sunny city was dandy, but they got back itchy and dusty.

3. Since Patty is handy, she can fix up that crummy shanty.

4. Sherry is very happy to be twenty today!

5. Yesterday they gave us plenty of yummy cherry candy.

6. You will do well if you copy Jerry's study habits.

Write:

1. _____

2. _____

    _____

3. _____

4. _____

5. _____

6. _____

Listen and write:

1. _____

2. _____

3. _____

4. _____

Sound: ly

chilly

The **ly** sound rhymes with the word **he**.

Read: ly   ly   ly   ly   ly   ly   ly   ly   ly   ly   ly   ly   ly   ly   ly   ly

Write: _____

Listen and write: _____

COMPARE

Read: ly   y   he   ly   she   ly   pull   le   ly   y   le   ly   y   le   ly   y   he

        ly   y   he   ly   she   ly   pull   le   ly   y   le   ly   y   le   ly   y   he

Write: _____

_____

Listen and write: _____

_____

WORDS

Read syllables: Write syllables: Read words: Write words twice:

1. chil   **ly**   chil __ ly   chilly   *chilly*   *chilly*
2. sad   **ly**   _____ _____   sad**ly**   _____   _____
3. bad   **ly**   _____ _____   bad**ly**   _____   _____
4. mad   **ly**   _____ _____   mad**ly**   _____   _____
5. jol   **ly**   _____ _____   jol**ly**   _____   _____
6. fol   **ly**   _____ _____   fol**ly**   _____   _____

Listen and write:

1. _____   4. _____   7. _____   10. _____

2. _____   5. _____   8. _____   11. _____

3. _____   6. _____   9. _____   12. _____

Sentences Using Words with the **ly** Ending

Additional words with the **ly** ending:

da**lly**	She**lly**	Po**lly**	prim**ly**	placi**dly**
ra**lly**	sme**lly**	du**lly**	simp**ly**	timi**dly**
Sa**lly**	chi**lly**	gu**lly**	gent**ly**	instant**ly**
be**lly**	go**lly**	ug**ly**	stiff**ly**	di**lly**da**lly**
Ke**lly**	ho**lly**	dim**ly**	grand**ly**	fu**lly***
Ne**lly**	Mo**lly**	grim**ly**	frank**ly**	

Read:

1. Frankly, I think it is silly of them to dillydally so long.
2. Molly gently said to Mr. Kelly, "Are you as chilly as I am?"
3. Instantly, but stiffly, Polly ran to the gully.
4. Shelly sadly sat at the rally amid the jolly kids.
5. Golly, this cabin is as smelly as it is ugly!
6. Nelly grimly said that she simply cannot go today.

Write:

1. _____

_____

2. _____

_____

3. _____

4. _____

5. _____

6. _____

Listen and write:

1. _____

2. _____

3. _____

4. _____

_____

***Fully** is a sight word.

Review: Words with le, al, y, ly

Read: le   al   pull   y   ly   he   le   al   pull   y   ly   he

Write: _____

Listen and
write: _____

COMPARE

le	y		
1. candle	candy	Write each word:	

candle   *candy*

le	y		
2. handle	handy	_____	_____
3. cattle	catty	_____	_____
4. battle	batty	_____	_____

le	ly		
		Write each word:	
5. gentle	gently	_____	_____
6. fondle	fondly	_____	_____
7. saddle	sadly	_____	_____

al	ly		
		Write each word:	
8. dismal	dismally	_____	_____
9. mental	mentally	_____	_____
10. central	centrally	_____	_____
11. comical	comically	_____	_____

Listen and write:

1. _____	4. _____	7. _____	10. _____
2. _____	5. _____	8. _____	11. _____
3. _____	6. _____	9. _____	12. _____

Review: Sentences Using Words with **le**, **al**, **y**, **ly**

Read:

1. When Kelly is in the saddle, he can handle the cattle.
2. Central to Jerry's dismal plan is a silly mock battle!
3. In this hospital, we handle the mentally ill very gently.
4. You think Sally is comical, but I think she is catty and fickle.
5. Did Willy put the candle in the middle of a candy dish?
6. Fondly, they snuggle the gentle puppy.
7. Bobby grimly put the metal thimble in the filthy bundle.
8. Polly simply cannot grapple with the shops in the capital city.

Write:

1. _____

_____

2. _____

_____

3. _____

_____

4. _____

_____

5. _____

_____

6. _____

_____

7. _____

_____

8. _____

_____

Listen and write:

1. _____

_____

2. _____

_____

3. _____

_____

4. _____

_____

5. _____

_____

6. _____

_____

7. _____

_____

8. _____

_____

9. _____

_____

10. _____

_____

11. _____

_____

12. _____

_____

Special Skill

PREVIEWING WORDS OF THREE OR MORE SYLLABLES FROM THE STORY The Dance Academy's Festival

Remember that each syllable has one vowel sound.

Read syllables:	Read words:	Write the words:
1. a cad e my	academy	<u>academy</u>
2. blue ber ry	blueberry	
3. bot tle brush	bottlebrush	
4. bot tle neck	bottleneck	
5. clas si cal	classical	
6. com i cal	comical	
7. com pe tent	competent	
8. con fi dent	confident	
9. cran ber ry	cranberry	
10. ex cel lent	excellent	
11. fes ti val	festival	
12. gel a tins	gelatins	
13. hos pi tal i ty	hospitality	
14. ma rim ba	marimba	
15. me tal lic	metallic	
16. ped es tal	pedestal	
17. piv ot al	pivotal	
18. prin ci pal	principal	
19. prom i nent	prominent	
20. sen ti men tal	sentimental	

Read syllables:	Read words:	Write the words:
21. splen did ly	splendidly	_____
22. tact ful ly	tactfully	_____
23. tim id ly	timidly	_____

Names and Places

24. Cas si dy	Cassidy	_____
25. Don nel son	Donnelson	_____
26. Ken ne dy	Kennedy	_____
27. Mex i can	Mexican	_____

Listen and write:

1. _____   13. _____
2. _____   14. _____
3. _____   15. _____
4. _____   16. _____
5. _____   17. _____
6. _____   18. _____
7. _____   19. _____
8. _____   20. _____
9. _____   21. _____
10. _____   22. _____
11. _____   23. _____
12. _____   24. _____

Story 8

Read: **The Dance Academy's Festival**

Peggy Kimble is the principal of a dance academy. Since she is so competent   1
and confident, she will set up the academy's dance festival. The budget has plenty of
cash for a potluck, too. This is not a brunch; it will happen on Saturday at 6 p.m. But
today something is amiss with Peggy. She is as jumpy as can be. She asks herself,
"Can I do this festival? Can I handle the hassle? Is it folly for me to grapple with
it?" She is in a muddle. Many men and women will come to the festival. Some of
them are prominent in the city. For a second, Peggy's mind boggles at the task, but
nothing stops her! She will do this project splendidly.

Today is the day of the festival. What a dismal day! It is chilly, foggy, and   2
misty. A drizzle dampens the city, too. The women and men bundle up and set off for
the academy. The academy is in the middle of the city. It is central to public transit
and the shuttle bus from the ferry. Some come at twenty past six. They got stuck in a
traffic bottleneck at the bridge to the ferry.

When they get to the academy, the lobby has a musty smell. It is full of   3
puddles that trickle off the wet jackets. But the men and women become as happy as if
it were a sunny day. The academy's setup for the festival is simple. It is dimly lit
with candles. The red and green holly and bottlebrush plants on the mantel dazzle
them. Bubbles come from the middle of the punch, which sits on a metallic pedestal.

Since it is a potluck, the women and men give something to Peggy. Jerry   4
Quimby has chops and chicken drumsticks to sizzle on the grill. Shelly Kennedy has
cherry candy. Perry Cassidy has crusty French buns. Polly and Wendel Mitty give
Peggy a bundle of pretzels. Rusty Kendal has brittle candy with nuts; it crackles as
you snap it into bits. Kitty Drexel-Bell has dill pickles. Kathy Mendel has cranberry
gelatins. Sherry and Rusty Donnelson have sixty blueberry muffins. Lily Bendel has

blueberry flapjacks for the griddle. Kerry Whipple has tonic in twenty bottles with nozzles. The things the men and women give are ample. At this potluck, they will have plenty of very yummy and excellent things to sample and nibble on. And Peggy has the kettle on, and it is hot!

Peggy got a dance band for the festival. They can do classical, rock, and ethnic hits. They do jazz and minstrel ballads, too. They have fiddles, a kettledrum, timbals, rattles, and a glossy marimba.   **5**

The band begins with the lindy. Some women and men dance madly and are very nimble. They jiggle and wiggle as they dance. At the signal, they do the bunny hop. It is a funny, frisky dance, and very comical. Next, they do the Mexican hat dance. They clap briskly and jump as the band jiggles the rattles. Then some do a belly dance. They swiftly do pivotal twists of the hips. They deftly shimmy as pals giggle.   **6**

Henry, a husky man, wants to dance very badly, but sits primly, timidly, and stiffly. Nelly thinks fondly of Henry. She is in her best frilly dress. She asks him to dance. "Do not be a fuddy-duddy, Henry," she said gently. "Will you dance with me?"   **7**

"Frankly, Nelly, I cannot dance," Henry said. "I am clumsy. I just wobble."

"I will give you a lesson, Henry," said Nelly softly. "This is the hully gully. You can do it." Then she adds tactfully, "With the hully gully, you can wobble as much as you want!"

Henry said with a happy grin, "I will gamble on that and dance with you. But you must not tattle if I trample you!"

At the end of the festival, some men and women dance the fox-trot to a sentimental hit. They snuggle and cuddle. They are happy.   **8**

At 12 midnight, the festival ends. It is a pity. The women and men are groggy. Some rally to help Peggy pick up the messy things. Then, sadly, they go. They thank Peggy for her hospitality. This festival at the dance academy did not fizzle. It was simply grand!   **9**

Story 8 emphasizes:
* endings with **le, al, y, ly**

and includes selections from:
* two-syllable, short-vowel words and names
* verb + **s** (third-person singular); noun + **'s** (possessive)
* special sounds: **ck, sh, ch, tch, th, wh, ce, ci, ge, gi, dge**
* initial and final blends
* sight words: **for, or, want, too, women, today, yesterday, was, were, thing, nothing, think, thank, what, from**
* three or more syllable words: **academy, blueberry, bottlebrush, bottleneck, classical, comical, competent, confident, cranberry, excellent, festival, gelatins, hospitality, marimba, metallic, pedestal, pivotal, principal, prominent, sentimental, splendidly, tactfully, timidly**
* three- and four-syllable names: **Cassidy, Donnelson, Kennedy, Mexican**

Sound: **ing**

ring

Read: ing   ing   ing   ing   ring   sing   king   ing   ing   ing

Write: _____

Listen and
write: _____

COMPARE

Read: ing   y   ly   ing   y   ly   ing   y   ly   ing   y   ly
            y   ing   ly   ly   ing   y   ing   y   ly   ing   ly   y

Write: _____

_____

Listen and
write: _____

_____

WORDS

Read: Write: Read: Write:

1. **ring**   _____   7. s**ting**   _____

2. s**ing**   _____   8. th**ing**   _____

3. w**ing**   _____   9. sw**ing**   _____

4. k**ing**   _____   10. Ch**ing**   _____

5. d**ing**   _____   11. fl**ing**   _____

6. p**ing**   _____   12. br**ing**   _____

Listen and write:

1. _____   4. _____   7. _____   10. _____

2. _____   5. _____   8. _____   11. _____

3. _____   6. _____   9. _____   12. _____

Sentences Using **ing** Nouns

Additional words with **ing**:

noth**ing***	**Ling**-**Ling**	**Ming**
someth**ing***	**Ping**-**Pong**	**Bing**
Flush**ing**	sh**ing**le	Lex**ing**ton

Read:

1.   Nothing will stop her from visiting Lexington.
2.   It is costly, but that Ming gem is something she must have!
3.   A little robin with brown wings was singing to the king.
4.   If you fling the shingles to him, they will sting his hands!
5.   Has Mr. Ching had a Bing cherry yet?
6.   Did Ling-Ling bring her kids to Flushing today?

Write:

1.   _____
2.   _____
3.   _____
4.   _____
5.   _____
6.   _____

Listen and write:

1.   _____
2.   _____
3.   _____
4.   _____
5.   _____
6.   _____

*These are sight words. In the first syllable of each word, **o** = **ŭ** (**sun**).

Adding **ing** to Verbs

If a verb ends in two consonants, just add **ing**:

Read: Write the **ing** word:

1. pack   + ing   = pa**ck**ing   *packing*

2. fish   + ing   = fi**sh**ing   _____

3. slant   + ing   = sla**nt**ing   _____

4. jump   + ing   = ju**mp**ing   _____

If a verb ends in just one consonant, double that consonant before adding **ing**:

Read: Write the **ing** word:

1. run + n + ing   = ru**nn**ing   _____

2. sit + t + ing   = si**tt**ing   _____

3. nap + p + ing   = na**pp**ing   _____

4. wag + g + ing   = wa**gg**ing   _____

Write the **ing** form of these verbs. Where needed, double the consonants:

Read: Write the **ing** word:

1. che**ck**   *checking*

2. get   _____

3. tra**p**   _____

4. pu**sh**   _____

5. jo**g**   _____

6. sta**nd**   _____

7. fla**sh**   _____

8. cra**m**   _____

Read and write these **ing** verbs.

Read:	Add **ing**:		Write:
1. pi**ck**	**ing**	pic**king**	pick ing picking
2. ba**ck**	**ing**	bac**king**	
3. dock	ing	docking	
4. kick	ing	kicking	
5. tick	ing	ticking	
6. rock	ing	rocking	
7. peck	ing	pecking	
8. duck	ing	ducking	
9. pack	ing	packing	
10. catch	ing	catching	
11. hitch	ing	hitching	
12. match	ing	matching	
13. pitch	ing	pitching	
14. hatch	ing	hatching	
15. patch	ing	patching	
16. itch	ing	itching	
17. wish	ing	wishing	
18. fish	ing	fishing	
19. cash	ing	cashing	
20. dash	ing	dashing	
21. shell	ing	shelling	
22. dish	ing	dishing	
23. rush	ing	rushing	
24. mash	ing	mashing	

Read: Add **ing**:   Write:

25. crash   ing   crashing   _____ ____ _____

26. trash   ing   trashing   _____ ____ _____

27. stash   ing   stashing   _____ ____ _____

28. flash   ing   flashing   _____ ____ _____

29. smack   ing   smacking   _____ ____ _____

30. stack   ing   stacking   _____ ____ _____

31. slack   ing   slacking   _____ ____ _____

32. quack   ing   quacking   _____ ____ _____

33. stand   ing   standing   _____ ____ _____

34. brand   ing   branding   _____ ____ _____

35. twitch   ing   twitching   _____ ____ _____

36. stitch   ing   stitching   _____ ____ _____

Listen and write:

1. _____   11. _____   21. _____

2. _____   12. _____   22. _____

3. _____   13. _____   23. _____

4. _____   14. _____   24. _____

5. _____   15. _____   25. _____

6. _____   16. _____   26. _____

7. _____   17. _____   27. _____

8. _____   18. _____   28. _____

9. _____   19. _____   29. _____

10. _____   20. _____   30. _____

Doubling a Consonant to Form **ing** Verbs

If a verb ends in one consonant, double the consonant before adding **ing**. For example:

Read:

				Write:
1. run	**n**	**ing**	ru**nning**	<u>run</u> <u>n</u> <u>ing</u> <u>running</u>

Read:

Write:

1. run	**n**	ing	ru**nning**	_____ __ ___ _____
2. sit	t	ing	sitting	_____ __ ___ _____
3. pat	t	ing	patting	_____ __ ___ _____
4. fit	t	ing	fitting	_____ __ ___ _____
5. win	n	ing	winning	_____ __ ___ _____
6. bat	t	ing	batting	_____ __ ___ _____
7. can	n	ing	canning	_____ __ ___ _____
8. fan	n	ing	fanning	_____ __ ___ _____
9. tag	g	ing	tagging	_____ __ ___ _____
10. nap	p	ing	napping	_____ __ ___ _____
11. chat	t	ing	chatting	_____ __ ___ _____
12. chop	p	ing	chopping	_____ __ ___ _____
13. ship	p	ing	shipping	_____ __ ___ _____
14. shop	p	ing	shopping	_____ __ ___ _____
15. snap	p	ing	snapping	_____ __ ___ _____
16. slap	p	ing	slapping	_____ __ ___ _____
17. cram	m	ing	cramming	_____ __ ___ _____
18. slam	m	ing	slamming	_____ __ ___ _____
19. jab	b	ing	jabbing	_____ __ ___ _____

Listen and write:

1. _____   3. _____   5. _____

2. _____   4. _____   6. _____

Adding **ing** to Verbs with **to be**

Add **ing** to the verb and use the correct form of **to be**.

to pack	
I pack	we pack
you pack	you pack
he packs	they pack
she packs	
it packs	

to be (today)	
I am	we are
you are	you are
he is	they are
she is	
it is	

to be (yesterday)	
I was	we were
you were	you were
he was	they were
she was	
it was	

Today (present)

Read:

1. I am packing.

2. You are packing.

3. He is packing.

4. She is packing.

5. It is packing.

6. We are packing.

7. You are packing.

8. They are packing.

Write:

I am packing.

_____

_____

_____

_____

_____

_____

_____

Yesterday (past)

Read:

1. I was packing.

2. You were packing.

3. He was packing.

4. She was packing.

5. It was packing.

6. We were packing.

7. You were packing.

8. They were packing.

Write:

I was packing.

_____

_____

_____

_____

_____

_____

_____

Sentences Using **ing** Verbs

Read:

1. Was he rushing to do his shopping?
2. Is she thinking of cashing her check today?
3. The robin is sitting on the bench and pecking at a nut.
4. She is pitching, he is batting, and I am catching.
5. Tim is picking up the logs and putting them on the deck.
6. They are canning shellfish at the packing plant.
7. Were the quacking ducks swimming in the pond?
8. Are you planning on doing some singing and dancing?

Write:

1. _____
2. _____
3. _____
    _____
4. _____
5. _____
    _____
6. _____
7. _____
8. _____
    _____

Listen and write:

1. _____
2. _____
3. _____

Special Skill: Adding **ing** to Verbs

Add **ing** to the verb in parentheses under the blank. Double the consonant if the verb ends in only one consonant. Look at these examples:

a. I am *rushing* to the shed.
(rush)

b. They are *patting* the dog.
(pat)

Read and write:

1. We are _____ the clams.
(can)

2. Are they _____ the dresses?
(fit)

3. I am _____ the nuts.
(shell)

4. She is _____ the lemons.
(ship)

5. Ching is _____ the cups.
(fill)

6. You are _____ the pants.
(stitch)

7. I am _____ the box.
(shut)

8. We are _____ the truck.
(pack)

9. Ling-Ling is _____ on the dock.
(fish)

10. He is_____ the logs.
(chop)

11. Are we _____ to the picnic?
(go)

12. They are _____!
(win)

Sound: ang

angry

Read: ang   ang   ang   ang   ang   ang   ang   ang   ang   ang

Write: _____

Listen and
write: _____

COMPARE

Read: ang   ing   ang   and   ing   ang   ing   ang   ing   ang

        and   ang   ant   ang   ing   ang   ast   ang   act   ang

Write: _____

_____

Listen and
write: _____

_____

WORDS

Read: Write:

1. **ang**ry _____

2. b**ang** _____

3. f**ang** _____

4. g**ang** _____

5. h**ang** _____

6. L**ang** _____

Read: Write:

7. p**ang** _____

8. r**ang** _____

9. s**ang** _____

10. t**ang** _____

11. cl**ang** _____

12. spr**ang** _____

Listen and write:

1. _____   4. _____   7. _____   10. _____

2. _____   5. _____   8. _____   11. _____

3. _____   6. _____   9. _____   12. _____

Sentences Using Words with **ang**

Additional words with **ang**:

W**ang**	tw**ang**	j**ang**le	g**ang**ly
Y**ang**	**ang**le	m**ang**le	h**ang** back
Ch**ang**	b**ang**le	t**ang**le	h**ang** on
sl**ang**	d**ang**le	sp**ang**le	h**ang** up

Read:

1. At 12 noon, Chang rang the lunch bell.

2. Hang up that satin dress with the bangles and spangles.

3. The angry animals have fangs that can mangle.

4. In the band, some sang and some hit the drums with a clang!

5. Miss Lang felt a pang of sadness.

6. The gangly kid sprang up. Will he dangle on the branch?

Write:

1. _____

2. _____

3. _____

4. _____

5. _____

6. _____

Listen and write:

1. _____

2. _____

3. _____

4. _____

5. _____

6. _____

Sound: **ong**

ping-pong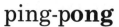

Read: ong   ong   ong   ong   ong   ong   ong   ong   ong   ong

Write: _____

Listen and
write: _____

COMPARE

Read: ong   ing   ang   ong   ing   ang   ong   ond   ong   ing

       ong   oft   ong   olf   ong   ang   ong   ing   ong   ang

Write: _____

_____

Listen and
write: _____

_____

WORDS

Read:	Write:	Read:	Write:
1. ping-p**ong**	_____	7. th**ong**s	_____
2. s**ong**	_____	8. bel**ong**	_____
3. l**ong**	_____	9. al**ong**	_____
4. g**ong**	_____	10. str**ong**	_____
5. W**ong**	_____	11. pr**ong**	_____
6. t**ong**s	_____	12. m**ong**rel	_____

Listen and write:

1. _____   4. _____   7. _____   10. _____

2. _____   5. _____   8. _____   11. _____

3. _____   6. _____   9. _____   12. _____

Sentences Using Words with **ong**

Additional words with **ong**:

Hong Kong   **Fong**   ding**ong**

Read:

1.   Is Mr. Wong going to sing the song or hit the gong?
2.   Put the Ping-Pong paddle back and come along with us.
3.   Did you get the sandals with thongs in Hong Kong?
4.   Are the long tongs with the big prongs still on the grill?
5.   That strong mongrel dog belongs to me.
6.   A long dingdong rings when Mrs. Fong swings the metal bell.

Write:

1.   _____
2.   _____
3.   _____
4.   _____
5.   _____
6.   _____

Listen and write:

1.   _____
2.   _____
3.   _____
4.   _____
5.   _____
6.   _____

Sound: **ung, eng**   lung    **leng**th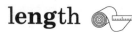

Read: ung   eng   ung   eng   ung   ung   eng   eng   ung   eng

Write: _____

Listen and
write: _____

COMPARE

Read: ung   eng   ing   ung   ang   eng   ong   ung   ing   eng

        ung   ong   eng   ing   ung   ang   eng   ong   ung   ing

Write: _____

_____

Listen and
write: _____

_____

WORDS

Read: Write: Read: Write:

1. **lung**   _____   7. **clung**   _____

2. **leng**th _____   8. **flung**   _____

3. h**ung**   _____   9. sl**ung**   _____

4. r**ung**   _____   10. st**ung**   _____

5. s**ung**   _____   11. sw**ung**   _____

6. Ch**ung**   _____   12. h**ung**ry _____

Listen and write:

1. _____   4. _____   7. _____   10. _____

2. _____   5. _____   8. _____   11. _____

3. _____   6. _____   9. _____   12. _____

Sentences Using Words with **ung**, **eng**

Additional words with **ung**:

m**ung**	**fung**us	**tung**sten
b**ung**le	str**ung**	**lung**fish
d**ung**	shant**ung**	k**ung** fu*
Ch**ung**		

Additional words with **eng**:

stren**g**th
England**
English**

Read:

1. A fungus is a plant, but tungsten is a metal.
2. I swung at the big bug just as it stung me!
3. We flung the dung into the ditch to get rid of it.
4. With her strong lungs, she will not bungle that song.
5. The hungry kid clung to his hot lunch.
6. They had sung a song in English, then they strung up the flag.

Write:

1. _____
2. _____
3. _____
4. _____
5. _____
6. _____

Listen and write:

1. _____
2. _____
3. _____
4. _____
5. _____
6. _____

---

*Fu rhymes with **blue**.
Eng sounds like **ing in these words.

Review: Comparing **ing**, **ang**, **ong**, **ung**, **eng**

Read:

	ing	ang	ong	ung	eng
1.	sing	sang	song	sung	
2.	Bing	bang	bong	bungle	
3.	Ling	Lang	long	lung	length
4.	mingle	mangle	mongrel	mung	
5.	string	strangle	strong	strung	strength
6.	tingle	tangle	tong	tungsten	

Write each word in the correct column:

	ing	ang	ong	ung	eng
1.	sing	sang	song	sung	
2.					
3.					
4.					
5.					
6.					

Listen and write:

	ing	ang	ong	ung	eng
1.					
2.					
3.					
4.					
5.					
6.					

Review: Sentences Using Words with **ing**, **ang**, **ong**, **ung**, **eng**

Read:

1. Chung will hang the Ping-Pong net its full length.
2. Yesterday Wang sang a long song. Will Fung sing today?
3. The bell that she rang hung on a long string.
4. Ying has the strength to bring the tungsten tongs to Dr. Lang.
5. The robin sang and clung to a strong branch at the spring.
6. Fungus sprang up along the ring of rocks.

Write:

1. _____

    _____

2. _____

    _____

3. _____

    _____

4. _____

    _____

5. _____

    _____

6. _____

    _____

Listen and write:

1. _____

2. _____

3. _____

Sound: ink

sink

Read: ink   ink   ink   ink   ink   ink   ink   ink   ink

Write: _____

Listen and
write: _____

COMPARE

Read: ink   ank   ing   ink   ank   ing   ink   int   ing   ink
         ind   ank   ing   ink   ank   ing   ink   ank   ing   ink

Write: _____

_____

Listen and
write: _____

_____

WORDS

Read: Write: Read: Write:

1. s**ink**   _____   7. dr**ink**   _____

2. l**ink**   _____   8. bl**ink**   _____

3. m**ink**   _____   9. cl**ink**   _____

4. p**ink**   _____   10. pl**ink**   _____

5. r**ink**   _____   11. sl**ink**   _____

6. w**ink**   _____   12. th**ink**   _____

Listen and write:

1. _____   4. _____   7. _____   10. _____

2. _____   5. _____   8. _____   11. _____

3. _____   6. _____   9. _____   12. _____

Sentences Using Words with **ink**

Additional words with **ink**:

inkling	b**rink**	t**rink**et
inkstand	st**ink**	c**rink**le
inkwell	sh**rink**	

Read:

1. At the sink, you can fill his glass with a drink.
2. The mink ran across the rink as quick as a wink.
3. Will this cotton cloth crinkle and shrink in the hot tub?
4. Is she fixing the links on her little trinket?
5. That ink in the inkwell stinks!
6. If you blink, you will miss the pink bubbles.

Write:

1. _____
2. _____
3. _____
4. _____
5. _____
6. _____

Listen and write:

1. _____
2. _____
3. _____
4. _____
5. _____
6. _____

Sound: ank

ankle

Read: ank   ank   ank   ank   ank   ank   ank   ank   ank   ank

Write: _____

Listen and
write: _____

COMPARE

Read: ank   ink   ank   and   ank   ang   ank   and   ang   ink

       ank   and   ang   ack   ank   ing   and   ank   ang   and

Write: _____

       _____

Listen and
write: _____

       _____

WORDS

Read:	Write:	Read:	Write:
1. **ank**le	_____	7. y**ank**	_____
2. b**ank**	_____	8. th**ank**	_____
3. d**ank**	_____	9. dr**ank**	_____
4. r**ank**	_____	10. pr**ank**	_____
5. s**ank**	_____	11. bl**ank**	_____
6. t**ank**	_____	12. fl**ank**	_____

Listen and write:

1. _____   4. _____   7. _____   10. _____

2. _____   5. _____   8. _____   11. _____

3. _____   6. _____   9. _____   12. _____

Sentences Using Words with **ank**

Additional words with **ank**:

crank	**Hank**	**blank**et
cranky	**plank**	**thank**ful
tankful	**ank**let	**tank** top
rankle	**Rank**in	**blank** check
		blanket stitch

Read:

1. The lanky kid was cranky, so she had a nap on her blanket.
2. At the bank, Hank got some blank checks.
3. Did Mrs. Rankin get a tankful of gas?
4. Do the anklets on her ankle have gems in them?
5. When you thank him, do not yank his hand!
6. He drank the rank-smelling drink.

Write:

1. _____
2. _____
3. _____
4. _____
5. _____
6. _____

Listen and write:

1. _____
2. _____
3. _____
4. _____
5. _____
6. _____

Sound: **onk**

honk

Read: onk   onk   onk   onk   onk   onk   onk   onk   onk   onk

Write: _____

Listen and write: _____

COMPARE

Read: onk   ong   onk   ank   onk   ink   onk   ong   onk   ank

       onk   ink   ank   ink   onk   ong   ank   ink   onk   ong

Write: _____

_____

Listen and write: _____

_____

WORDS

Read: Write: Read: Write:

1. **h**onk _____   4. **cl**onk _____

2. **c**onk _____   5. **T**onk**in** Gulf _____

3. **b**onk _____   6. **h**onk**y-t**onk _____

Listen and write:

1. _____   4. _____   7. _____   10. _____

2. _____   5. _____   8. _____   11. _____

3. _____   6. _____   9. _____   12. _____

Sentences Using Words with **onk**

Read:

1.   When the cab got stuck, it kept honking to get help.
2.   Mr. Wong asked Hank to do a honky-tonk song.
3.   He did not conk his ankle on the edge of that plank!
4.   Will you fix this clonking clock so it will tick?
5.   The rocks went clonk, clonk as they fell.
6.   Did she bonk her skull on the bricks?

Write:

1.   _____
2.   _____
3.   _____
4.   _____
5.   _____
6.   _____

Listen and write:

1.   _____
2.   _____
3.   _____
4.   _____
5.   _____
6.   _____

Sound: **unk, enk**

trunk

Read: unk   unk   enk   unk   unk   enk   enk   unk   unk   unk

Write: _____

Listen and
write: _____

COMPARE

Read: unk   ung   enk   eng   ank   onk   ink   enk   unk   onk

            unk   ink   ank   onk   enk   ung   onk   ank   ink   ung

Write: _____

_____

Listen and
write: _____

_____

WORDS

Read: Write:

1. tr**unk**   _____

2. **Jenk**ins   _____

3. b**unk**   _____

4. d**unk**   _____

5. h**unk**   _____

6. j**unk**   _____

Read: Write:

7. s**unk**   _____

8. ch**unk**   _____

9. dr**unk**   _____

10. fl**unk**   _____

11. pl**unk**   _____

12. sk**unk**   _____

Listen and write:

1. _____   4. _____   7. _____   10. _____

2. _____   5. _____   8. _____   11. _____

3. _____   6. _____   9. _____   12. _____

Sentences Using Words with **unk**, **enk**

Additional words with **unk:**

funk	**lunk**	**junk**et
funky	**clunk**	**drunk**en
punk	**stunk**	**bunk** bed
sunken	**Strunk**	**punk** rock
gunk		

Read:

1. Angry skunks stunk up the cabin!
2. Can I dunk the chunks of muffin in the hot drink?
3. His kids think that punk rock is funky.
4. The Jenkins twins have bunk beds.
5. If we go on that junket, can we lug the big trunk?
6. Her sunken van had thick gunk stuck on it.

Write:

1. _____
2. _____
3. _____
4. _____
5. _____
6. _____

Listen and write:

1. _____
2. _____
3. _____
4. _____
5. _____
6. _____

Review: Comparing **ink, ank, onk, unk, enk**

Read:

	ink	ank	onk	unk	enk
1.	clink	clank	clonk	clunk	Jenkins
2.	plink	plank	plonk	plunk	
3.	sink	sank		sunk	
4.		Hank	honk	hunk	
5.	stink	stank		stunk	
6.	drink	drank		drunk	
7.	think	thank			

Write each word in the correct column:

	ink	ank	onk	unk	enk
1.	clink	clank	clonk	clunk	Jenkins
2.					
3.					
4.					
5.					
6.					
7.					

Listen and write:

	ink	ank	onk	unk	enk
1.					
2.					
3.					
4.					
5.					
6.					
7.					

Review:
Sentences Using Words with **ink**, **ank**, **onk**, **unk**, **enk**

Read:

1. The pet skunk just stunk up the sink!
2. That lanky kid has a lot of spunk!
3. He drank the drink that he had drunk yesterday.
4. Get the pink blanket off the trunk in the attic.
5. Do you think you will thank them for the trinket?
6. Get off the brink of that rotten plank!
7. If you want to get rid of this junk, sell it to Mr. Jenkins.
8. Stop winking and blinking at them, you big lunk!

Write:

1. _____

2. _____

3. _____

    _____

4. _____

    _____

5. _____

    _____

6. _____

    _____

7. _____

    _____

8. _____

    _____

Listen and write:

1. _____

_____

2. _____

_____

3. _____

_____

4. _____

_____

5. _____

_____

6. _____

_____

7. _____

_____

8. _____

_____

9. _____

_____

10. _____

_____

11. _____

_____

12. _____

_____

Special Skill

PREVIEWING WORDS WITH THREE OR MORE SYLLABLES FROM THE STORY The Franklin Fish Packing Plant

Remember that each syllable has one vowel sound.

Read syllables:	Read words:	Write the words:
1. ben e fit ing	benefiting	_____
2. fam i ly	family	_____
3. fin ish es	finishes	_____
4. fin ish ing	finishing	_____

Listen and write:

1. _____   3. _____

2. _____   4. _____

FORMING ing WORDS FROM le WORDS

le word		drop the e, add ing		pronounce in two syllables	ing word
1. giggle	→	giggl + ing	→	gig gling	giggling
2. handle	→	handl + ing	→	han dling	handling
3. mangle	→	mangl + ing	→	man gling	mangling
4. bungle	→	bungl + ing	→	bun gling	bungling

Read and write the words:

1. giggling _____   3. mangling _____

2. handling _____   4. bungling _____

Listen and write:

1. _____   3. _____

2. _____   4. _____

Story 9

Read: **The Franklin Fish Packing Plant**

Yung Chang is going to his job. He has a job at the Franklin Fish Packing   **1**
Plant. His boss is telling Yung what he has to do today. The boss is giving him a list
of tasks. He will be doing lots of things on this job. He will be checking the things off
as he finishes them.

Checklist for Packing Fish

_____ 1. **skinning the fish**
_____ 2. **putting the skin into a trash can**
_____ 3. **slitting the fish up the back**
_____ 4. **dropping the guts, gills, and fins into the trash can**
_____ 5. **chopping the fish into chunks**
_____ 6. **bagging the fish**
_____ 7. **stacking and chilling the fish**

Yung will be standing at a sink or sitting on a bench and cutting on a long   **2**
plank. He has a lot of strength.

As Yung is cutting, he is singing a song and thinking that this job at the   **3**
fish packing plant is not so bad. He is glad to be doing something for himself and his

family. They have just come from Hong Kong and are benefiting from his job. Yung Chang is cutting the fins off the fish and tossing them into a basket. Yung is putting some of the fish chunks into plastic bags. He is twisting the tops of the bags shut and stuffing them into hemp sacks. Then he is stamping **FRANKLIN FISH** on the sacks.

Yung Chang is sitting next to Ingrid Rankin. She is shelling clams, mussels, and shrimp. Ingrid is giggling at the song that Yung is humming. She is bagging and tagging her fish with the **FRANKLIN FISH** stamp, too. As Yung and Ingrid are finishing the packing job, Langston Bendel is coming to get the full hemp sacks from them. Langston is pushing a dolly. His job is in shipping. He is strong and is running and crashing along. Ingrid and Yung are grinning. They are betting that Langston will hit something. But Langston is coming to a full stop and not bumping a thing.   **4**

Langston and Yung are pals. Langston is telling Yung that he wants to go on a fishing trip. He is asking Yung to go with him. Yung is yelling at Langston, "No, no, no! I am not willing to go fishing! I do not want to be thinking of, smelling, or handling fish on a day off!"   **5**

Langston is grinning, "So, you want nothing to do with fishing since you have this job at the Franklin Fish Packing Plant! You have a hang-up!"   **6**

Then Yung is asking Langston, "Are you going to help me with tacking up some shingles on the shed? If you do, when we finish we can go jogging or have a Ping-Pong match."   **7**

Langston is telling Yung, "I will be ringing you up to tell you. Well, it was fun chatting with you, but I have to be going to docking." Langston is pushing the dolly with the sacks to the truck at the docking spot.   **8**

Linda King and her husband Hank do the trucking for the Franklin Fish Packing Plant. With Langston's help, they are dragging the sacks off the docking spot and flinging them into a truck for shipping. They are jumping up and lifting them, too. They are not mangling the sacks or bungling the job. Hank and Linda are doing the job well.   **9**

Inga Jenkins has a job at the fish packing plant, too. Her job is canning the fish. She is putting the fish into a big black kettle with long tongs until the fish gets hot. The plant is getting hot, too. Inga is glad she has a tank top and thongs on but no stockings. Stan Cassidy is sticking tags on the cans and stacking them in boxes with the **FRANKLIN FISH** stamp. As Stan is ending his job, Langston is rushing to get the boxes. After gabbing with Inga and Stan, Langston is bringing the boxes to the Kings.   **10**

They are grabbing the boxes, rushing to the truck, and cramming them in the full length of the truck. They are dashing off. In passing, they are thanking Langston for helping.

The shift is ending. What a hectic day at the Franklin Fish Packing Plant!   **11** The clock is ticking. On the job, men and women are packing up things. The boss is checking the last of the canning and tagging. Langston is locking up the shipping dock. As the bell is ringing, the women and men of the fish packing plant are punching the clock and going.

Story 9 emphasizes:
• **ing, ang, ong, ung, eng, ink, ank, onk, unk, enk**

and includes selections from:
• two-syllable, short-vowel words and names
• verb + **s** (third-person singular); noun + **'s** (possessive)
• special sounds: **ck, sh, ch, tch, th, wh, ce, ci, ge, gi, dge**
• initial and final blends
• other endings: **le, al, y, ly**
• sight words: **for, or, want, too, women, today, yesterday, was, were, nothing, what, from**
• three- and four-syllable words: **benefiting, family, finishes, finishing**

Sound: **ed = id**

The **ed** ending makes three different sounds:

> 1. **ed = id (lid)**
> 2. **ed** = d (dig)
> 3. **ed** = t (bit)

1. **ed** = **id** (as in **lid**)

Read: ed   ed   ed   ed   ed   ed   ed   ed   ed   ed   ed   ed

Write: _____

Listen and
write: _____

COMPARE

Read: ed   id   bid   hid   ed   kid   ed   bid   ed   did   ed
       id   ed   id   ed   did ed   bid ed   kid ed   hid

Write: _____

_____

Listen and
write: _____

_____

WORDS

Read:		Write:		Read:	Write:
1. land	**ed**	land ed		land**ed**	*landed*
2. sift	**ed**	_____ _____		sift**ed**	_____
3. blend	**ed**	_____ _____		blend**ed**	_____
4. add	**ed**	_____ _____		add**ed**	_____
5. mend	**ed**	_____ _____		mend**ed**	_____
6. last	**ed**	_____ _____		last**ed**	_____

Listen and write:

1. _____   3. _____   5. _____

2. _____   4. _____   6. _____

Special Skill: Spelling Words with the **ed** Ending

A. SHORT-VOWEL WORDS ENDING IN TWO OR MORE CONSONANTS

When a short-vowel word ends in **two or more** consonants, just add **ed** to spell the past tense. (See the six words on the previous page.) It is the same principle as adding **ing** (see page 137). For example:

Read: Write the **ed** word:

la**nd** + **ed** = la**nded**   _____

si**ft** + **ed** = si**fted**   _____

B. SHORT-VOWEL WORDS ENDING IN ONE CONSONANT

When a short-vowel word ends in only **one** consonant, that consonant must be doubled before adding **ed.** For example:

Read: Write the **ed** word:

ba**t** + **t** + **ed** = ba**tted**   _____

pa**d** + **d** + **ed** = pa**dded**   _____

Practice adding **ed** to short-vowel words ending in one consonant.

Read: Write the **ed** word twice:

 1. mat + **t** + **ed** = ma**tted**   *matted*   *matted*

 2. pat + t + ed = pa**tted**   _____   _____

 3. net + t + ed = ne**tted**   _____   _____

 4. pit + t + ed = pi**tted**   _____   _____

 5. gut + t + ed = gu**tted**   _____   _____

 6. glut + t + ed = glu**tted** _____   _____

 7. nod + d + ed = no**dded**   _____   _____

 8. plod + d + ed = plo**dded** _____   _____

 9. bed + d + ed = be**dded**   _____   _____

10. kid + d + ed = ki**dded**   _____   _____

11. shred + d + ed = shre**dded** _____   _____

Sentences Using Words with **ed** = **id**

Read:

1. Edwin sanded the deck and sodded the grass.
2. Wilma sifted the nutmeg and added the lemon.
3. Melvin patted the kitten's matted back.
4. The blimp plodded along, then landed with a thud.
5. We netted the fish, then gutted and shredded them.
6. I kidded with her until she batted.
7. Ned fitted the dress and mended the vest.

Write:

1. _____

   _____

2. _____

   _____

3. _____

   _____

4. _____

   _____

5. _____

   _____

6. _____

   _____

7. _____

   _____

Listen and write:

1. _____

2. _____

Sound: **ed = d**

Remember that the **ed** ending makes three different sounds:

$$\begin{cases} 1. & \textbf{ed} = \text{id (lid)} \\ 2. & \textbf{ed} = \textbf{d (dig)} \\ 3. & \textbf{ed} = \text{t (bit)} \end{cases}$$

2. **ed = d** (as in **dig**)

Read: ed   ed   ed   ed   ed   ed   ed   ed   ed   ed   ed   ed

Write: _____

Listen and write: _____

COMPARE

Read:
ed	d	filled	d	billed	d	chilled	id	landed
id	added	ed	d	bagged	d	pinned	d	trimmed

Write: _____

_____

Listen and write: _____

_____

WORDS

Read:		Write:	Read:	Write:
1. fill	**ed**	fill ed	fill**ed**	filled
2. bill	**ed**	_____ ___	bill**ed**	_____
3. chill	**ed**	_____ ___	chill**ed**	_____
4. bag g	**ed***	_____ ___	bag**ged**	_____
5. pin n	**ed***	_____ ___	pin**ned**	_____
6. trim m	**ed***	_____ ___	trim**med**	_____

Listen and write:

1. _____   3. _____   5. _____

2. _____   4. _____   6. _____

---

*Double the final consonant, then add **ed.**

Sentences Using Words with **ed** = **d**

Additional words in which **ed** sounds like **d**:

gagg**ed**	bann**ed**	spinn**ed**	cull**ed**	gabb**ed**	cramm**ed**	fell**ed**
lagg**ed**	cann**ed**		dull**ed**	nabb**ed**	ramm**ed**	smell**ed**
sagg**ed**	fann**ed**	kill**ed**	hull**ed**	grabb**ed**	brimm**ed**	well**ed**
tagg**ed**	mann**ed**	mill**ed**	lull**ed**	robb**ed**		
wagg**ed**	tann**ed**	till**ed**	mull**ed**	lobb**ed**	fizz**ed**	
dragg**ed**		frill**ed**		hobnobb**ed**	whizz**ed**	
		drill**ed**	pull**ed***			

Read:

1. She sagged, so Tom filled her glass with a chilled drink.
2. Chen bagged some apples yesterday and canned them today.
3. They grilled the chops and mulled the drinks.
4. Ann trimmed the hedges and tilled the land, then she billed them.
5. When the muck welled up, he smelled it and gagged.
6. He pinned the frilled dress that dragged, then he tagged it.

Write:

1. _____

   _____

2. _____

   _____

3. _____

   _____

4. _____

   _____

5. _____

   _____

6. _____

   _____

---

*This is a sight word.

Sound: ed = t

Remember that the **ed** ending makes three different sounds:

$$\begin{cases} 1. \ \textbf{ed} = \text{id (lid)} \\ 2. \ \textbf{ed} = \text{d (dig)} \\ 3. \ \textbf{ed} = \textbf{t (bit)} \end{cases}$$

3. **ed** = **t** (as in **bit**)

Read: ed   ed   ed   ed   ed   ed   ed   ed   ed   ed   ed   ed

Write: _____

Listen and
write: _____

COMPARE

Read: ed   t   jumped   t   missed   t   masked   t   hopped   t

stopped   t   mapped   t   ed   t   jumped   t   mashed   t

Write: _____

_____

Listen and
write: _____

_____

WORDS

Read:		Write:		Read:	Write:
1. jump	ed	_____	____	jumped	_____
2. miss	ed	_____	____	missed	_____
3. mask	ed	_____	____	masked	_____
4. hop p	ed*	_____	____	hopped	_____
5. stop p	ed*	_____	____	stopped	_____
6. map p	ed*	_____	____	mapped	_____

Listen and write:

1. _____   3. _____   5. _____

2. _____   4. _____   6. _____

---

*Double the final consonant, then add **ed.**

Sentences Using Words with **ed** = **t**

Additional words in which **ed** sounds like **t**:

bopp**ed**	pump**ed**	lack**ed**	mix**ed**	press**ed**	bunch**ed**	cuff**ed**
mopp**ed**	clump**ed**	sack**ed**	danc**ed**	stitch**ed**	hunch**ed**	huff**ed**
sopp**ed**	slump**ed**	tack**ed**	lanc**ed**	ditch**ed**	lunch**ed**	fluff**ed**
topp**ed**	trump**ed**	hock**ed**	pranc**ed**	hitch**ed**	punch**ed**	bluff**ed**
bump**ed**	push**ed***	lock**ed**	glanc**ed**	latch**ed**	brunch**ed**	stuff**ed**
dump**ed**	bush**ed***	sock**ed**	bless**ed**	match**ed**	crunch**ed**	ripp**ed**
hump**ed**	back**ed**	kiss**ed**	mess**ed**	thatch**ed**	buff**ed**	tripp**ed**
lump**ed**	hack**ed**	fix**ed**	dress**ed**	munch**ed**		

Read:

1. The rabbit hopped and jumped but missed the basket.
2. We stopped and lunched with Wilma at the thatched inn.
3. He ripped his pants, so Mom stitched and pressed them.
4. They mapped the trip and hitched up the wagon.
5. He was sad, but masked it with a grin and danced.
6. When the van was fixed, I pumped gas into it and locked it up.

Write:

1. _____

   _____

2. _____

   _____

3. _____

   _____

4. _____

   _____

5. _____

   _____

6. _____

   _____

---

*These are sight words. The **u** sounds like the **u** in **pull**.

Review: Sound Chart of Short-Vowel Words Ending in ed

Read the root words and the past-tense words ending in **ed**. Compare the sounds of the **ed** words in the three groups.

Notice that the root words in each group end in different sounds.

Group Ending Sounds

1. t, d
2. r, l, v, m, b, g, n, e, z
3. p, k, s, sh, ch, f

1. **ed = id**		2. **ed = d**		3. **ed = t**	
bat	batted	enter	entered	hop	hopped
pat	patted	banter	bantered	help	helped
fit	fitted	clutter	cluttered	chop	chopped
pit	pitted	shutter	shuttered	shop	shopped
flit	flitted			nap	napped
visit	visited	fill	filled	chap	chapped
last	lasted	chill	chilled	stop	stopped
blast	blasted	shell	shelled	ship	shipped
plant	planted	mull	mulled	jump	jumped
chat	chatted				
spot	spotted	live**	lived	pack	packed
melt	melted			stack	stacked
expect	expected	slam	slammed	tick	ticked
invest	invested	cram	crammed	click	clicked
butt	butted	trim	trimmed	check	checked
glut	glutted	hum	hummed	shuck	shucked

1. ed = id

add	added
pad	padded
plod	plodded
land	landed
sand	sanded
end	ended
mend	mended
blend	blended
bond	bonded
fund	funded

2. ed = d

jab	jabbed
mob	mobbed
club	clubbed
bag	bagged
tag	tagged
beg	begged
hug	hugged
can	canned
pin	pinned
plan	planned
shun	shunned
study*	studied
buzz	buzzed
fizz	fizzed
whiz	whizzed

3. ed = t

miss	missed
pass	passed
dance**	danced
fence**	fenced
fix***	fixed
mix***	mixed
fuss	fussed
finish	finished
wish	wished
famish	famished
crash	crashed
brush	brushed
hatch	hatched
stitch	stitched
fetch	fetched
crunch	crunched
buff	buffed
stuff	stuffed
whiff	whiffed

---

*Change the **y** to **i** and add **ed**.

If the root word ends in **e, just add **d**.

***Do not double the **x** before adding **ed**.

Listen and write:

1. _____   26. _____   51. _____

2. _____   27. _____   52. _____

3. _____   28. _____   53. _____

4. _____   29. _____   54. _____

5. _____   30. _____   55. _____

6. _____   31. _____   56. _____

7. _____   32. _____   57. _____

8. _____   33. _____   58. _____

9. _____   34. _____   59. _____

10. _____   35. _____   60. _____

11. _____   36. _____   61. _____

12. _____   37. _____   62. _____

13. _____   38. _____   63. _____

14. _____   39. _____   64. _____

15. _____   40. _____   65. _____

16. _____   41. _____   66. _____

17. _____   42. _____   67. _____

18. _____   43. _____   68. _____

19. _____   44. _____   69. _____

20. _____   45. _____   70. _____

21. _____   46. _____   71. _____

22. _____   47. _____   72. _____

23. _____   48. _____   73. _____

24. _____   49. _____   74. _____

25. _____   50. _____   75. _____

Review: Short-Vowel Words Ending in **ed**

Add the **ed** ending to each of these root words.* Either add **ed** alone or double the consonant if necessary. For example:

back   *backed*   bat   *batted*

Read the root word. Write the root word with its **ed** ending.

Read:	Write:	Read:	Write:
pat	_____	dance	_____
flit	_____	fix	_____
last	_____	finish	_____
plant	_____	hatch	_____
melt	_____	crunch	_____
expect	_____	buff	_____
invest	_____	hop	_____
butt	_____	fill	_____
pad	_____	live	_____
plod	_____	slam	_____
fund	_____	jab	_____
blend	_____	beg	_____
help	_____	can	_____
shop	_____	study	_____
jump	_____	buzz	_____
pack	_____	whiz	_____
miss	_____	enter	_____

---

*Watch out for exceptions. Some root words need only **d** added to form the past tense. For example: *fence → fenced*

Listen and write:

Root Word

1. _____
2. _____
3. _____
4. _____
5. _____
6. _____
7. _____
8. _____
9. _____
10. _____
11. _____
12. _____
13. _____
14. _____
15. _____
16. _____
17. _____
18. _____
19. _____
20. _____
21. _____
22. _____
23. _____
24. _____
25. _____

Word with *ed* ending

26. _____
27. _____
28. _____
29. _____
30. _____
31. _____
32. _____
33. _____
34. _____
35. _____
36. _____
37. _____
38. _____
39. _____
40. _____
41. _____
42. _____
43. _____
44. _____
45. _____
46. _____
47. _____
48. _____
49. _____
50. _____

Review: Sentences with Words Ending in ed

Remember that the **ed** ending can sound like **id**, **d**, or **t**.

Read:

1. As she shelled the nuts, he pitted and chopped the plums.
2. Insects buzzed as they planted the elm and fenced in the pond.
3. What he planned for ended when the stocks he invested in crashed.
4. She added the frilled, backless dress to the packed trunk.
5. Mr. and Mrs. Edison chatted, hummed, and kissed as they danced.
6. As we expected, he lived in the unfinished cabin and fixed it up.
7. When she finished swimming, she felt chilled and put on her padded, quilted jacket.
8. When she visited Florida, she crammed in a trip to Tampa but missed the Gulf.

Write:

1. _____

    _____

2. _____

    _____

3. _____

    _____

4. _____

    _____

5. _____

    _____

6. _____

    _____

7. _____

    _____

8. _____

    _____

Listen and write:

1. _____

_____

2. _____

_____

3. _____

_____

4. _____

_____

5. _____

_____

6. _____

_____

7. _____

_____

8. _____

_____

9. _____

_____

10. _____

_____

11. _____

_____

12. _____

_____

Special Skill

PREVIEWING WORDS WITH THREE OR MORE SYLLABLES
FROM THE STORY We Visited Uncle Ned's Cattle Ranch

Remember that each syllable has one vowel sound.

Read syllables:	Read words:	Write the words:
1. ac com plished	accomplished	*accomplished*
2. a dapt ed	adapted	
3. ad mit ted	admitted	
4. an i mals	animals	
5. as ton ished	astonished	
6. bud get ed	budgeted	
7. bul let ed	bulleted	
8. col lect ed	collected	
9. dif fi cult	difficult	
10. dif fi cul ty	difficulty	
11. em bed ded	embedded	
12. ex it ed	exited	
13. ex pect ed	expected	
14. fan tas tic	fantastic	
15. fidg et ed	fidgeted	
16. hos pi tal i ty	hospitality	
17. in vest ed	invested	
18. jack rab bits	jackrabbits	
19. pos si ble	possible	
20. spir it ed	spirited	
21. tal ent ed	talented	
22. un ex pect ed ly	unexpectedly	
23. up com ing	upcoming	
24. vis it ed	visited	

Listen and write:

1. _____
2. _____
3. _____
4. _____
5. _____
6. _____
7. _____
8. _____
9. _____
10. _____
11. _____
12. _____
13. _____
14. _____
15. _____
16. _____
17. _____
18. _____
19. _____
20. _____
21. _____
22. _____
23. _____
24. _____
25. _____

26. _____
27. _____
28. _____
29. _____
30. _____
31. _____
32. _____
33. _____
34. _____
35. _____
36. _____
37. _____
38. _____
39. _____
40. _____
41. _____
42. _____
43. _____
44. _____
45. _____
46. _____
47. _____
48. _____
49. _____
50. _____

Story 10

Read: **We Visited Uncle Ned's Cattle Ranch**

Mom and Dad had invested in a split-level. Mom, Dad, Fred, and I expected to   **1**
be happy in it. We had trimmed the hedges, sodded the land, sanded the deck, and
fixed up the kitchen. We wanted things to be tip-top. Then, unexpectedly, Dad's
Uncle Ned asked us to visit him at his Angus cattle ranch in Kansas. We cherished
Uncle Ned. We wanted to visit him badly. We longed to go! So we planned and
mapped the trip. Fred and I begged to have Red, the dog, come along, too. Dad and
Mom said, "Yes!"

We glumly admitted that we had to pack up some of the stuff we had just   **2**
unpacked. Dad grinned and said, "So what! Let nothing stop us from going." We
budgeted for it and cashed in some bonds. Mom kept a bulleted list of things to do. We
checked them off as we finished doing the tasks.

Dad rented a van from a man with a tag pinned on the pocket of his jacket. He   **3**
said, "You will be billed for renting it when you come back." We filled the van with
lots of things. We packed things in trunks, boxes, and duffel bags. We crammed in as
much stuff as possible. We dumped kitchen things in a box, stuffed blankets and

bedding into duffel bags, then packed jackets and denim pants (some patched) into a trunk, which we locked. We tagged the trunks with Uncle Ned's address since we wanted them shipped to his ranch. We left them to be picked up on the split-level's back steps. When we were finished tagging the trunks, we lugged the boxes and duffel bags to the deck and stacked them up. The boxes were so full that they thudded as they landed! Then we dragged the boxes and duffel bags to the van and lifted them into it. When we were finished, we latched the van.

The packing lasted a full day, which was too long for us! It was a very difficult   **4**
day. We were unskilled and lacked a lot of strength. What a day! Fred got so hot that he fanned himself with his cap. We gagged on the dust. We felt hassled and frazzled, but we kidded as we plodded along and kept at it. We tackled the job and finished it well. In fact, we were astonished at what we had accomplished.

At the end of the day, we chuckled at some of the funny (and not so funny)   **5**
things that had happened to us, such as:

—Dad backed up the van and bumped into the deck. Then he banged his hip as he   **6**
   hopped off the van! Mom jested, "You are sacked, but I cannot let you quit until we
   have finished." Dad said, "You win, boss! I will not quit until I have helped you."

—Fred tripped on a rug and bumped into a lamp. The lamp crashed and cracked into a   **7**
   hundred little bits.

—Mom dropped a potted plant when Red jumped up and licked her neck. The pet was   **8**
   banished to the deck, but the dog did not go until he was fed and petted.

—Dad filled a trash bag and dumped it into the trash can, but the bag ripped. The   **9**
   trash missed the can, spilled onto the mat, and messed up the kitchen.

—I slipped on the trash, skidded, and did a split as I fell. They clapped and said that I   **10**
   was talented. I yelled at them to shut up as I rubbed black-and-blue legs and
   mopped the kitchen.

We discussed and planned the upcoming trip, then plopped into bed at 8 p.m.   **11**
We slept until 8 a.m. the next day! We got up and dressed. We donned pressed and mended pants and jackets. Fred cuffed his fitted pants and slicked himself up. He strutted to the van. I kidded him. "Do you think you are a ranch hand?" I said. We

got into the van and buckled up. It was jam-packed, and were we cramped! But we were off to Uncle Ned's ranch! We glanced back at the split-level. It was locked up.

A full day had passed when we got to the exit for the ranch. We signaled as we **12** exited from the ramp. Then we angled left at the bend to Uncle Ned's ranch. We were very impressed with it. The ranch's fenced-in grassland went on and on. It all smelled fresh. Uncle Ned welcomed us. We settled in quickly. The men and women ranch hands were glad to have us and helped us. We children bunked with the ranch hands; Mom and Dad lodged with Uncle Ned.

Uncle Ned had lots of animals. We were somewhat inept with them, but we **13** got skilled at it. We punched cattle, milked the stock, fed the chickens, and tended the kids. Fred and I patted and petted them. Uncle Ned bred pigs and hogs, too. We fattened the penned-in animals with cobs. They grunted at us! Eggs hatched into little chicks. We collected the unhatched eggs and candled them.

Uncle Ned bred Angus cattle on his ranch. They were very strong! Uncle's **14** best bull was Teddy. He had a polished brass ring that dangled from his nostrils. Uncle Ned tipped us off to the fact that Teddy was handled with difficulty. He stressed that we must do nothing to get the bull mad!

Teddy was so spirited that we wanted to get on him. We plotted to do it. One **15** day, we snuck into the fenced-in ring. Teddy got miffed! The bull panted, huffed, and puffed at us. As fast as can be, we dashed from the bull and jumped the fence. Uncle Ned yelled, "You tangled with Teddy! A kid can be mangled doing that!" Fred and I fidgeted, but Uncle Ned did not punish us. He said that we had been punished running from a maddened bull!

We helped with the tasks at the ranch. Uncle Ned drilled a well, and we **16** pumped and filled buckets from it. We tilled and mulched the land and dug up embedded rocks. We planted some crops and thinned them back. At Uncle Ned's grist mill, we threshed, hulled, and milled. We picked plums and canned them. We felled a big elm and chopped it into logs. We chopped so much that we dulled the ax! We fished in the pond as green-necked ducks swam.

One day we saddled up, hitched up some wagons, and camped on the grassland **17** with Uncle Ned and the ranch hands. Jed fed us from the chuck wagon. We gobbled up the grilled chops and settled on the grass. Jackrabbits hopped as we sat. Bucks pranced in the distance. The ranch hands fiddled and sang ballads. Some of them gossiped and chatted with us. They impressed us with ranch legends.

A lot happened to us when we visited Uncle Ned at his cattle ranch. We **18** adapted well to the ranch. At the end of the day, we were bushed and wilted. We hobbled off to bed, but we were very happy. The visit strengthened us, and we felt fulfilled.

At the end of the visit, sadness welled up in us. As we left, we thanked Uncle **19** Ned for his hospitality. Uncle Ned said that we had helped him a lot. It was a fantastic visit! Uncle Ned and the ranch hands hugged and kissed us. They wished us well and said, "You will be missed!" Uncle Ned added, "I was blessed that you visited me. Come back to the ranch!"

Story 10 emphasizes:
- **ed** past-tense endings with three different sounds (**id, d, t**)

and includes selections from:
- two-syllable, short-vowel words and names
- verb + **s** (third-person singular); noun + **'s** (possessive)
- special sounds: **ck, sh, ch, tch, th, wh, ce, ci, ge, gi, dge**
- initial and final blends
- other endings: **le, al, y, ly, ing, ang, ong, ung, eng, ink, ank, onk, unk, enk**
- sight words: **for, or, want, too, women, today, yesterday, was, were, nothing, what, from**
- three- or more syllable words (see list on page 181)

Sound: er

runner

This ending can be added to a word to show that a person or thing is doing an action.

Read: er   er   er   er   er   er   er   er   er   er   er

Write: _____

Listen and
write: _____

COMPARE

Read: er   ed (id)   ed (d)   ed (t)   er   ed (id)   ed (d)   ed (t)

    er   ed (id)   ed (d)   ed (t)   er   ed (id)   ed (d)   ed (t)

Write: _____

_____

Listen and
write: _____

_____

WORDS*

Read syllables: Write syllables: Read words:* Write the words twice:

1. run   **ner** run ner   runner   *runner   runner*

2. sand   **er** _____ _____   sand**er**   _____ _____

3. drill   **er** _____ _____   drill**er**   _____ _____

4. pitch **er** _____ _____   pitch**er**   _____ _____

5. jump **er** _____ _____   jump**er**   _____ _____

6. bat   **ter** _____ _____   bat**ter**   _____ _____

Listen and write:

1. _____   4. _____   7. _____   10. _____

2. _____   5. _____   8. _____   11. _____

3. _____   6. _____   9. _____   12. _____

—————

*See page 192 for spelling rules.

Sentences Using Words with **er**

Read and compare: Write:

1. Nick can jump.   _____

    He is a jumper.   _____

2. Beth can sand.   _____

    She is a sander.   _____

3. Kevin can drill.   _____

    He is a driller.   _____

4. Donna can pitch.   _____

    She is a pitcher.   _____

5. Chuck can run.   _____

    He is a runner.   _____

6. Anna can bat.   _____

    She is a batter.   _____

Listen and write:

1. _____

2. _____

3. _____

4. _____

5. _____

6. _____

7. _____

8. _____

9. _____

10. _____

11. _____

12. _____

Special Skill

er AT THE END OF A WORD = NOUN

Read words:	Write words:	Read words:	Write words:
1. hammer	_____	7. dinner	_____
2. bumper	_____	8. supper	_____
3. lodger	_____	9. locker	_____
4. butter	_____	10. shopper	_____
5. sitter	_____	11. checker	_____
6. zipper	_____	12. thinker	_____

Listen and write:

1. _____

2. _____

3. _____

4. _____

5. _____

6. _____

SENTENCES

Read:

1. His hammer is in a locker.
2. Her van has a big bumper.
3. The lodger has dinner at the inn.
4. A thinker will do well on this exam.
5. The sitter had supper with the little kids.
6. Did the checker put the butter and the zipper in the shopper's bag?

Write:

1. _____

2. _____

3. _____

4. _____

5. _____

6. _____

Special Skill
er AT THE END OF A WORD = ADJECTIVE

Read words: Write words:

1. better   _____

2. fatter   _____

3. quicker   _____

4. thicker   _____

5. flatter   _____

6. longer   _____

Read words: Write words:

7. bigger   _____

8. thinner   _____

9. faster   _____

10. damper   _____

11. hotter   _____

12. madder   _____

Listen and write:

1. _____

2. _____

3. _____

4. _____

5. _____

6. _____

SENTENCES

Read:

1. This dish is flatter and thicker than that cup.
2. Today it is damper and hotter than yesterday.
3. The fatter the hen, the bigger the eggs are.
4. The quicker the swimmer, the faster the laps will be.
5. The thinner he is, the madder he gets!
6. Karen is a better runner than I am since she has longer legs.

Write:

1. _____

2. _____

3. _____

4. _____

5. _____

6. _____

Listen and write:

1. _____

2. _____

3. _____

4. _____

5. _____

6. _____

7. _____

8. _____

9. _____

10. _____

11. _____

12. _____

13. _____

14. _____

15. _____

16. _____

17. _____

18. _____

19. _____

20. _____

21. _____

22. _____

23. _____

24. _____

Special Skill

SPELLING WORDS WITH THE er ENDING
A. Short-Vowel Words Ending in Two or More Consonants

Words ending in **er** are formed from the root word in two ways, similar to the way **ing** and **ed** words are formed (see pages 137 and 168). When a short-vowel word ends in two or more consonants, just add **er**. For example:

Read:

    le**nd** + **er** = le**nder**

    si**ft** + **er** = si**fter**

Write the **er** word:

_____

_____

B. Short-Vowel Words Ending in One Consonant

When the short-vowel word ends in only one consonant, that consonant must be doubled before adding **er**. For example:

Read:

    bat + **t** + **er** = ba**tter**

    win + **n** + **er** = wi**nner**

Write the **er** word:

_____

_____

Read:

1. rent + **er** = renter
2. bank + er = banker
3. bump + er = bumper
4. catch + er = catcher
5. check + er = checker
6. big + g + er = bigger
7. red + d + er = redder
8. zip + p + er = zipper
9. shop + p + er = shopper
10. swim + m + er = swimmer

Write the words twice:

renter   renter

_____ _____

_____ _____

_____ _____

_____ _____

_____ _____

_____ _____

_____ _____

_____ _____

_____ _____

Review: Chart of Words with **er**

glibber	under	bagger	dasher	banker	banner
blubber	fonder	tagger	masher	tanker	manner
	tender	begger	fisher	inker	tanner
amber	fender	bigger	crasher	tinker	dinner
member	lender	digger	flasher	honker	sinner
limber	mender	jigger	slasher	bunker	winner
timber	sender	jogger	fresher	franker	runner
lumber	blender	logger	crusher	blinker	
number	cinder	hugger		clinker	helper
slumber		slugger	backer	thinker	
	doer		packer		camper
cancer		anger	bicker	caller	damper
dancer	differ	hanger	dicker	seller	tamper
prancer	buffer	finger	locker	teller	temper
mincer	duffer	singer	rocker	biller	simper
pincer	suffer	longer	sucker	killer	bumper
officer	staffer	hunger	blacker	fuller	tramper
	bluffer	stinger	cracker	speller	whimper
adder	stuffer		stacker	driller	
ladder		larger	checker		pepper
madder	badger		clicker	gentler	dipper
bladder	ledger	catcher	quicker	littler	zipper
gladder	codger	etcher	sticker		upper
redder	dodger	pitcher	thicker	dimmer	supper
sledder	lodger	sketcher	trucker	simmer	shipper
bidder				summer	skipper
kidder				glimmer	clipper
				shimmer	flipper
				slimmer	slipper
				swimmer	chopper
				trimmer	shopper
				glummer	stopper

			Sight Words	**Longer Words**	**Colors**
dresser	batter	waxer	father	attacker	greener
presser	fatter	fixer	mother	hanger-on	whiter
	matter	mixer	brother	fender bender	bluer
after	latter	boxer	grandfather	litterbug	grayer
rafter	better		grandmother	litter basket	pinker
softer	letter			well-wisher	
	setter			gangster	
welter	bitter			prankster	
swelter	fitter			blockbuster	
	litter			shutterbug	
center	sitter				
renter	potter				
winter	butter				
planter	cutter				
	gutter				
faster	putter				
sister	glitter				
duster	fritter				
muster	blotter				
blister	plotter				
twister	clutter				
bluster	flutter				
cluster	shutter				
fluster	stutter				

Special Note:

One word can have many uses. For example, the word **better**:

We had **better** do it!   (adverb)

He can **better** himself in that job.   (verb)

She is a **better** singer than I am.   (adjective)

They will get the **better** of us and win.   (noun)

Write (or Listen and write):

1. _____

2. _____

3. _____

4. _____

5. _____

6. _____

7. _____

8. _____

9. _____

10. _____

11. _____

12. _____

13. _____

14. _____

15. _____

16. _____

17. _____

18. _____

19. _____

20. _____

21. _____

22. _____

23. _____

24. _____

25. _____

26. _____

27. _____

28. _____

29. _____

30. _____

31. _____

32. _____

33. _____

34. _____

35. _____

36. _____

37. _____

38. _____

39. _____

40. _____

41. _____

42. _____

43. _____

44. _____

45. _____

46. _____

47. _____

48. _____

49. _____

50. _____

51. _____

52. _____

53. _____

54. _____

55. _____

56. _____

57. _____

58. _____

59. _____

60. _____

61. _____

62. _____

63. _____

64. _____

65. _____

66. _____

67. _____

68. _____

69. _____

70. _____

71. _____

72. _____

73. _____

74. _____

75. _____

Review: Sentences with Three Kinds of **er** Words

Read:

1. Under stress, the pitcher is better than the catcher or the batter.
2. Grandmother, a limber jogger, is fonder of skim milk than butter.
3. The bank teller entered the numbers in the thinner ledger.
4. The runner's blister is redder today than it was yesterday.
5. Was the cab with the bigger rubber bumper in a fender bender?
6. Grandfather's well-bred setter just had a litter of seven pups!
7. A number of singers sang tender songs as well as blockbuster hits.
8. She was the faster swimmer and was under the bridge in a matter of seconds.

Write:

1. _____

   _____

2. _____

   _____

3. _____

   _____

4. _____

   _____

5. _____

   _____

6. _____

   _____

7. _____

   _____

8. _____

   _____

Listen and write:

1. _____

_____

2. _____

_____

3. _____

_____

4. _____

_____

5. _____

_____

6. _____

_____

7. _____

_____

8. _____

_____

9. _____

_____

10. _____

_____

11. _____

_____

12. _____

_____

Special Skill
PREVIEWING WORDS OF THREE OR MORE SYLLABLES
FROM THE STORY Mr. Webster's Day at the Bunker Hill Bank

Remember that each syllable has one vowel sound.

Read syllables:	Read words:	Write the words:
1. ad min is ters	administers	*administers*
2. af ter math	aftermath	
3. a gen da	agenda	
4. an oth er	another	
5. as sist ed	assisted	
6. blith er ing	blithering	
7. block bust er	blockbuster	
8. bob sled ders	bobsledders	
9. cal i ber	caliber	
10. cit i zens	citizens	
11. col lat er al	collateral	
12. con sid ered	considered	
13. cus tom ers	customers	
14. dis cuss es	discusses	
15. el der ly	elderly	
16. en cum ber	encumber	
17. es tab lish ment	establishment	
18. ex is tence	existence	
19. ex pect ed	expected	
20. ex ter nal	external	
21. fam i ly	family	
22. fed er al	federal	
23. fin ger tips	fingertips	
24. flut ter ing	fluttering	

Read syllables:	Read words:	Write the words:
25. for ev er	forever	_____
26. fra ter nal	fraternal	_____
27. gov ern ment	government	_____
28. grand fath er	grandfather	_____
29. grand moth er	grandmother	_____
30. han ker ing	hankering	_____
31. hap pi ly	happily	_____
32. he li cop ter	helicopter	_____
33. in her it ed	inherited	_____
34. in ter con ti nen tal	intercontinental	_____
35. in ter est	interest	_____
36. in ter nal	internal	_____
37. in ter pret ed	interpreted	_____
38. in ter rupt ed	interrupted	_____
39. in ter vals	intervals	_____
40. in vest ment	investment	_____
41. lav en der	lavender	_____
42. lib er al	liberal	_____
43. lim it ed	limited	_____
44. man ag er	manager	_____
45. of fi cer	officer	_____
46. pas sen ger	passenger	_____
47. per son al	personal	_____
48. per son nel	personnel	_____
49. prop er ly	properly	_____
50. prop er ty	property	_____
51. reg is tered	registered	_____
52. res i dents	residents	_____

Read syllables:	Read words:	Write the words:
53. sen ti nel	sentinel	
54. sev er al	several	
55. sus pect ed	suspected	
56. sus pend ers	suspenders	
57. ter rif ic	terrific	
58. to geth er	together	
59. trav el ers	travelers	
60. un der stand ing	understanding	
61. vet er an	veteran	
62. vis it ed	visited	
63. wind jam mer	windjammer	
64. won der ful	wonderful	
65. Al ber ta	Alberta	
66. A mer i can	American	
67. An der son	Anderson	
68. At lan tic	Atlantic	
69. Bev er ly	Beverly	
70. Em er son	Emerson	
71. Hen der son	Henderson	
72. Jen ni fer	Jennifer	
73. Nan tuck et	Nantucket	
74. Roch es ter	Rochester	
75. Swit zer land	Switzerland	
76. Van der hoff	Vanderhoff	
77. Win ches ter	Winchester	

Listen and write:

1. _____
2. _____
3. _____
4. _____
5. _____
6. _____
7. _____
8. _____
9. _____
10. _____
11. _____
12. _____
13. _____
14. _____
15. _____
16. _____
17. _____
18. _____
19. _____
20. _____
21. _____
22. _____
23. _____
24. _____
25. _____
26. _____
27. _____
28. _____
29. _____

30. _____
31. _____
32. _____
33. _____
34. _____
35. _____
36. _____
37. _____
38. _____
39. _____
40. _____
41. _____
42. _____
43. _____
44. _____
45. _____
46. _____
47. _____
48. _____
49. _____
50. _____
51. _____
52. _____
53. _____
54. _____
55. _____
56. _____
57. _____
58. _____

Story 11

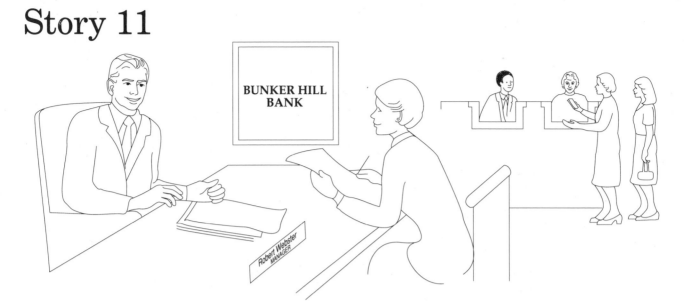

Read: **Mr. Webster's Day at the Bunker Hill Bank**

Robert Webster was a bank officer and the manager of the Bunker Hill Bank. **1**
He was a member of the establishment, too. Citizens of Bunker Hill asked Mr.
Webster, an investment planner and a lender, for help. Webster was no bungler. He
had the facts at his fingertips, and he passed them along to others. This was what the
public wanted from a banker. He was a problem-solver. The Bunker Hill Bank was
considered lucky to have a person of his caliber on the job.

Webster's mother and father wanted him to marry. He had been single longer **2**
than his brother, Roger, and Robert was the elder. But his mother and father were not
meddlers or naggers. They did not badger Robert when he visited them on
Nantucket. Since they lived on the Atlantic, they were avid swimmers. On some
days, they were golfers and joggers, too. They had a setter dog. No gentler dog than
Buster ever lived. He was no hunter and not much of a sentinel, but the Websters
were happy to have the big bluffer as a pet.

When Robert visited his mother and father, he traveled to and from Nantucket **3**
on a windjammer as a passenger. He was a chum of the skipper's. When Robert was
very rushed, he went in a helicopter, which was quicker.

His grandfather and grandmother were Emersons and lived in Amherst. He **4**
visited them a lot, too. His grandfather was a member of the clergy.

Today was Monday. Since it was much brisker and wetter than Sunday, **5**
Webster donned a muffler under his slicker. For him, to swelter under the summer
sun was better. But it was winter. He shivered, then quickly zippered up the slicker.
He had lavender suspenders on under his gray flannel jacket.

As Webster entered the Bunker Hill Bank, he was thinking that today was **6** much grayer than yesterday. He got to his desk, doffed his slicker and muffler, and hung them on a hanger. He glanced at the clock with the big black numbers. It was 7:50 a.m. At his signal at exactly 8 a.m., Chester Brenner and Hester Miller unlatched the locks and let the customers in. Hundreds flocked to the Bunker Hill Bank in a day. The bank's coffers were fuller than ever. The clatter in the bank went up to the rafters as the tellers helped the customers with checks, cash, and bank drafts. Customer Service assisted with the transfer of funds, mergers, interest, registered checks, and personal matters.

Beverly Anderson was a trust officer of the bank. She got today's agenda from **7** the printer and handed it to Robert. He glanced at it as they welcomed one another. Robert was thinking, "What a terrific staffer she is!" To Robert, Beverly was wonderful. On the job, she was quicker and faster than the rest of the top-level personnel. He grinned at Beverly as she said, "I have the ledgers for you, too, Mr. Webster." She put them on his blotter. "I have studied the letters of credit that you drafted yesterday. You are a better thinker than speller, but I interpreted them!" Beverly bantered with Robert. "Thank you, Miss Anderson," Robert said very properly. He had gotten fonder of her and wanted to tell her so. Beverly had a hankering for Robert, and she was single, too.

Some of Webster's long-term customers sat on the ladder-back benches as he **8** scanned his numbered agenda for the day:

Monday, December 30

1. Dr. and Mrs. Abner Gerber—want traveler's checks; $500 per person
2. Mr. and Mrs. Lester Henderson—truckers; want bank as backer
3. Miss Polly and Miss Abby Vanderhoff—want to fix up inherited property
4. Mr. Dexter Skinner—wants letter of credit

Then he met with the customers at intervals, some longer than others.

1. Abner and Alberta Gerber were elderly, but did not want to sit in rockers. **9** They were constant travelers. They had just come back from an intercontinental trip

to Switzerland. That day, they wanted traveler's checks. They had plans for a trip from Rochester to Denver and then back to Vermont. They were avid bobsledders, and this was a fun-filled winter for them.

2. Lester and Verna Henderson wanted the bank as a backer. Lester was a trucker and packer. Verna was a singer and dancer in supper clubs. She wanted to be Lester's helper. They wanted to expand to be bidders for and shippers of timber and lumber. They planned to pick up the lumber from docks along the rivers. They wanted to get tandem rigs.   **10**

The Hendersons had limited collateral, but Robert trusted them. They were long-term residents of Bunker Hill. They had some rental property as a tax shelter. They were thrifty. Lester was an American veteran with a lot of service. Lester was a boxer, so he was stronger than lots of men—a plus in trucking. They had two foster children: Jennifer, 11, and Spencer, 9. The Hendersons were planning to adopt the kids and wanted a better existence for the family. For Robert Webster, the clincher was a bumper sticker they had with them that said: **11**

The Hendersons Are **Number One** with Lumber

He wanted to back them 100 percent. He lent the Hendersons the funds in a manner that did not encumber them.

3. Miss Polly and Miss Abby Vanderhoff were elderly, well-to-do spinster sisters. They were fraternal twins that lived a sheltered existence. They had inherited family property in Winchester long ago. Herbert, the butler, was with the sisters. (He had served the Vanderhoff family since the sisters were children.) Miss Polly was a potter; Miss Abby was a sketcher of clipper ships. They wanted to convert the loft into an art center. The loft was cluttered with junk. They wanted the loft to be "modern." They wanted to fix up the gutters and do other external jobs on the property, too. Miss Polly said to Mr. Webster that she suffered from bladder, liver, and other internal problems (and whispered, "I'm thankful it's not cancer"). She added that she was hampered on steps, too. So they had to put in a lift to get her to the art center.   **12**

Miss Abby said to her sister, "Stop the blithering, Polly. Do not bother and pester the lad with problems of sickness." Then she said to Mr. Webster, "Sister gets flustered when she discusses funds, but she is a stickler for perfect results."   **13**

Webster administers the trust for the Vanderhoff sisters. He was understanding and had a liberal plan for them.   **14**

4. Dexter Skinner wanted a letter of credit. But Skinner had a pattern of **15** several bad investments and was bankrupt. He had had tax problems with the federal government; he was a spendthrift. He had a glib manner, too.

Robert suspected that Skinner was a gambler and perhaps a gangster. **16** Skinner suspected that Webster was on to him, so he said, "Rob, be a chum and help a buddy!" Webster interrupted him, "Mr. Skinner, you are on a faster track than this bank. We differ. We do not wish to dicker with you, but we must be franker than in the past. The Bunker Hill Bank can no longer be a backer for you. You have passed the upper limits of credit." Robert Webster was no sucker! He had gotten Skinner's number. Skinner was a credit risk. Skinner was bitter and vented his anger. "You have slandered me!" he yelled as he left the bank.

At the end of the day, Robert Webster asked Beverly Anderson to have dinner **17** with him at the Banker's Club. She said, "Yes!"

Dinner was perfect! Beverly and Robert had salad with fresh pepper, crackers **18** with butter, and lobster. For dessert, they had apple fritters in a crisp batter topped with sherbet. After dinner, they danced to songs on a zither under the Big Dipper. They lingered longer at the club than Robert had expected. Beverly said he was a grand dancer. When he held her hand, her fingers felt tender to him. He felt a fluttering in his chest. He was fonder of her than ever.

Robert said to himself, "Nothing can be better than being with Beverly." **19** Beverly asked herself, "What will the aftermath of this be?" If the two of them can be a little franker, they can marry and be together forever and "live happily ever after." Robert Webster's day was a blockbuster!

Story 11 emphasizes:
- words ending in **er**

and includes selections from:
- words ending in **le**, **al**, **y**, **ly**, **ing**, **ang**, **ong**, **ung**, **eng**, **ank**, **ink**, **onk**, **unk**, **enk**, **ed**
- two-syllable, short-vowel words and names
- verb + **s** (third-person singular); noun + **'s** (possessive)
- special sounds: **ck**, **sh**, **ch**, **tch**, **th**, **wh**, **ce**, **ci**, **ge**, **gi**, **dge**
- initial and final blends
- sight words: **for**, **or**, **want**, **too**, **women**, **today**, **yesterday**, **was**, **were**, **nothing**, **what**, **from**
- three or more syllable words and names (see list on pages 198-200)

CHAPTER 6:
Contractions and Special Sounds

In this chapter, you will read, write, compare, and review ways to shorten words and phrases by omitting letters and spaces and adding an apostrophe ('). You will learn to form the contractions

- ► **it's** (it is)
- ► **that's** (that is)
- ► **noun + 's** (such as **Beth's, man's, dog's, cab's**)
- ► **he's** (he is)
- ► **she's** (she is)
- ► **I'm** (I am)
- ► **isn't** (is not)
- ► **aren't** (are not)
- ► **wasn't** (was not)
- ► **weren't** (were not)
- ► **hasn't** (has not)
- ► **haven't** (have not)
- ► **can't** (cannot)

You also will learn these special sounds:

- ► **y = ĭ** (as in gym)
- ► **ive = ĭv** (as in live)
- ► **tion = shun** (as in mention)

In addition, you will read, write, and review sentences and stories that emphasize these lessons and contain some three or more syllable words.

Contractions Using 's: it is = **it's**

Use the **'s** contraction to make two words into one word that means the same thing. For example:

a. **It is** running. = **It's** running.

b. I think **it is** running. = I think **it's** running.

Read and compare:

| It is | It's | it is | it's | It is | It's | it is | it's |
| It is | It's | it is | it's | It is | It's | it is | it's |

Write: It is   It's _____

_____

Listen and
write: _____

_____

SENTENCES

Read and compare: Write:

1. **It is** a camel.   _____

   It's a camel.   _____

2. **It is** a big basket.   _____

   It's a big basket.   _____

3. **It is** a box of ribbons.   _____

   It's a box of ribbons.   _____

4. Dan thinks **it is** a fish.   _____

   Dan thinks **it's** a fish.   _____

5. If **it is** hot, I will go.   _____

   If **it's** hot, I will go.   _____

6. When you visit, **it is** fun.   _____

   When you visit, **it's** fun.   _____

Contractions Using 's: that is = **that's**

Use the **'s** contraction to make two words into one word that means the same thing. For example:

    a. **That is** running well. = **That's** running well.

    b. I think **that is** running well. = I think **that's** running well.

Read and compare:

That is	That's	that is	that's	That is	That's	that is
that's	That is	That's	that is	that's	That is	That's

Write: <u>That is   That's</u>

_____

Listen and
write: _____

_____

SENTENCES

Read and compare: Write:

1. **That is** a cat.   _____

   That's a cat.   _____

2. I think **that is** a dog.   _____

   I think **that's** a dog.   _____

3. **That is** hot!   _____

   That's hot!   _____

4. If **that is** her cup, fill it.   _____

   If **that's** her cup, fill it. _____

5. When **that is** full, mix it.   _____

   When **that's** full, mix it. _____

6. Fran thinks **that is** best.   _____

   Fran thinks **that's** best. _____

Contractions Using 's: *noun* is = ***noun*'s**

Use the **'s** contraction to make two words into one word that means the same thing. For example:

   a. The **man is** running. = The **man's** running.

   b. I think the **man is** running. = I think the **man's** running.

Read and compare:

The van is	The van's	an egg is	an egg's	The rip is	The rip's
The ant is	The ant's	a bat is	a bat's	Kim is	Kim's

Write:

The van is   The van's

_____

Listen and write:

_____

_____

SENTENCES

Read and compare: Write:

1. The **van is** running.   _____

    The **van's** running.   _____

2. An **egg is** missing.   _____

    An **egg's** missing.   _____

3. The **rip is** getting big.   _____

    The **rip's** getting big.   _____

4. The **ant is** a pest!   _____

    The **ant's** a pest!   _____

5. A **bat is** black.   _____

    A **bat's** black.   _____

6. **Kim is** glad.   _____

    Kim's glad.   _____

Contractions Using 's and 'm:
he is = **he's**, she is = **she's**, I am = **I'm**

Use the **'s** or **'m** contraction to make two words into one word that means the same thing. For example:

a. **He is** running. = **He's** running.
    She is running. = **She's** running.

b. I think **he is** running. = I think **he's** running.
    I think **she is** running. = I think **she's** running.

c. **I am** running. = **I'm** running.*
    I think **I am** running. = I think **I'm** running.

Read and compare:

He is   He's   he is   he's   She is   She's   she is   she's   I am   I'm

Write: _____

_____

Listen and
write: _____

_____

SENTENCES

Read and compare: Write:

1. **He is** a nasty kid.   _____

    He's a nasty kid.   _____

2. **She is** better at tennis.   _____

    She's better at tennis.   _____

3. **Chuck is** a jogger.   _____

    He's a jogger.   _____

4. **Brenda is** a swimmer.   _____

    She's a swimmer.   _____

5. Ann thinks **she is** a comic.   _____

    Ann thinks **she's** a comic.   _____

6. If **I am** well, I can go.   _____

    If **I'm** well, I can go.   _____

_____

*The **I** in **I am** and **I'm** is always capitalized.

Contractions with **not** = **n't**:
isn't, aren't, wasn't, weren't, hasn't, haven't, can't

Read words:	Read contractions:	Write the contractions twice:
1. is **not**	isn't	*isn't* *isn't*
2. are **not**	aren't	
3. was **not**	wasn't	
4. were **not**	weren't	
5. has **not**	hasn't	
6. have **not**	haven't	
7. cannot*	can't	

SENTENCES

Read and compare: Write:

1. An ant **is not** big.

   An ant **isn't** big.

2. Tankers **are not** little.

   Tankers **aren't** little.

3. The dancer **was not** limber.

   The dancer **wasn't** limber.

4. They **were not** members.

   They **weren't** members.

5. He **has not** studied.

   He **hasn't** studied.

6. We **have not** helped.

   We **haven't** helped.

7. She **cannot** swim.

   She **can't** swim.

*Cannot** is one word.

Listen and write:

1. _____

2. _____

3. _____

4. _____

5. _____

6. _____

7. _____

8. _____

9. _____

10. _____

11. _____

12. _____

13. _____

14. _____

15. _____

16. _____

17. _____

18. _____

19. _____

20. _____

21. _____

22. _____

23. _____

24. _____

Review: Contractions with **is** (**it's, that's, he's, she's, *noun*'s**); with **not** (**isn't, aren't, wasn't, weren't, hasn't, haven't, can't**) and with **am** (**I'm**)

Read and compare:

Write:

1. it is   it's   *it is*   *it's*

2. that is   that's

3. he is   he's

4. she is   she's

5. the man is   the man's

6. is not   isn't

7. are not   aren't

8. was not   wasn't

9. were not   weren't

10. has not   hasn't

11. have not   haven't

12. cannot   can't

13. I am   I'm

Read: Write the contractions:

1. is not   *isn't*

2. cannot

3. it is

4. were not

5. she is

6. have not

7. was not

8. the dog is

9. that is

10. are not

11. has not

12. he is

13. I am

Read: Write the full words:

I'm   *I am*

weren't

haven't

she's

it's

can't

hasn't

isn't

wasn't

that's

the shopper's

aren't

he's

Bonus Page
COMPLETING SENTENCES WITH CONTRACTIONS

it is= it's	she is = she's	was not = wasn't
that is = that's	I am = I'm	were not = weren't
noun is = *noun*'s	is not = isn't	has not = hasn't
he is = he's	are not = aren't	have not = haven't
		cannot = can't

Complete each sentence with the contraction of the words in parentheses ():

1. They _weren't_ moving to a split-level. (were not)

2. The Quinns _____ coming with us. (are not)

3. I think _____ too hot to go jogging. (it is)

4. _____ a happy person! (Nancy is)

5. He _____ got his check yet. (has not)

6. _____ her grandfather an artist? (Is not)

7. _____ a wonderful thing to say. Thank you! (That is)

8. We _____ go into the city today. (cannot)

9. _____ at her tennis lesson until noon. (She is)

10. They _____ visited with the family today. (have not)

11. _____ grilling chicken on the grill. (He is)

12. Vincent _____ concerned about the benefits. (was not)

13. _____ the best man at Nick and Beth's wedding! (I am)

Listen and write:

1. _____

2. _____

3. _____

4. _____

5. _____

6. _____

Sound: y = ĭ

gym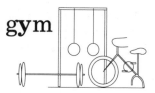

Read: y   y   y   y   y   y   y   y   y   y   y   y   y   y   y

Write: _____

Listen and
write: _____

COMPARE

Read: y   gym   gypsum   y   giblet   give   y   cyst   cinnamon   y

         myth   mince   y   Lynch   inch   y   gym   Jerry   city

Write: _____

         _____

Listen and
write: _____

         _____

WORDS

Read: Write: Read: Write:

1. gym   _____   7. Lynch   _____

2. gypsum   _____   8. myth   _____

3. cyst   _____   9. pyramid   _____

4. cynical _____   10. symptom   _____

5. cylinder _____   11. system   _____

6. symbol   _____   12. typical   _____

Listen and write:

1. _____   4. _____   7. _____   10. _____

2. _____   5. _____   8. _____   11. _____

3. _____   6. _____   9. _____   12. _____

Sentences Using Words with the y = ĭ sound

Additional words with the y = ĭ sound:

Two sounds of y
y = ĭ and y = ē:

cygnet	mystical	synopsis	styptic	dysentery
gymnast	syllable	syntax	abysmal	mystery
gymnastics	symbolic	synthetic	abyss	tyranny
gyp	symmetrical	syringe	analytic	symmetry
hypnotic	sympathetic	syrup	antonym	sympathy
hysterics	synergistic	systematic	Gladys	gypsy moth
Lynn	synod	tympanic	Dylan	
mystic	synonym	Flynn	Alyssa	

Read:

1. Lynn Lynch is an abysmal gymnast but a hypnotic dancer.
2. I'm cynical; is the gypsum in the cylinder synthetic?
3. Dr. Flynn said that a cyst is a typical symptom of that illness.
4. The mystery of the pyramids is filled with myths.
5. In that sentence, the synonyms and antonyms have many syllables.
6. The analytical staff was not sympathetic to the boss's hysterics and tyranny.

Write:

1. _____

2. _____

3. _____

4. _____

5. _____

6. _____

Sound: ive

give

The vowel in this sound sounds like **ĭ** as in **inch**.

Read: ive   ive   ive   ive   ive   ive   ive   ive   ive   ive

Write: _____

Listen and
write: _____

COMPARE

Read: ive   give   ive   live   ive   it   ive   sit   ive   cyst

       ive   gym   ive   live   ive   give   ive   it   ive   sit

Write: _____

_____

Listen and
write: _____

_____

WORDS

Read: Write: Read: Write:

1. give   _____   7. positive   _____

2. live   _____   8. negative   _____

3. active   _____   9. incentive   _____

4. massive   _____   10. expressive   _____

5. festive   _____   11. inventive   _____

6. objective   _____   12. perspective   _____

Listen and write:

1. _____   4. _____   7. _____   10. _____

2. _____   5. _____   8. _____   11. _____

3. _____   6. _____   9. _____   12. _____

Sentences Using Words with the **ive** Ending

Additional words with the **ive** ending:

passive	selective	attentive	subjective	pensive
missive	invective	compulsive	sensitive	extensive
expensive	offensive	relative	fixative	additive
elective	inductive	combative	permissive	infinitive
formative	impulsive	impressive	tentative	inquisitive

Read:

1. It's expensive to live in that city!
2. Give them extensive benefits as a job incentive.
3. Since he's so permissive, his kids are impulsive and offensive.
4. You were very selective when you got her that impressive gift!
5. Think positive, and you will stop being so negative!
6. Be objective with inquisitive relatives.

Write:

1. _____

2. _____
   _____

3. _____
   _____

4. _____
   _____

5. _____
   _____

6. _____

Listen and write:

1. _____

2. _____

Sound: **tion**

addi**tion**

$$\begin{array}{r} 1 \\ +2 \\ \hline 3 \end{array}$$

This sound sounds like **shun**.

Read: tion   tion   tion   tion   tion   tion   tion   tion   tion

Write: _____

Listen and
write: _____

COMPARE

Read: tion   shun   th   sh   tch   tion   shun   th   sh   tch

        shun   tion   sh   th   tion   tch   th   shun   tch   sh

Write: _____

_____

Listen and
write: _____

_____

WORDS

Read: Write: Read: Write:

1. addi**tion**   _____   7. suc**tion**   _____

2. men**tion**   _____   8. inten**tion**   _____

3. sec**tion**   _____   9. convic**tion**   _____

4. ac**tion**   _____   10. conven**tion**   _____

5. condi**tion**   _____   11. attri**tion**   _____

6. fic**tion**   _____   12. attrac**tion**   _____

Listen and write:

1. _____   4. _____   7. _____   10. _____

2. _____   5. _____   8. _____   11. _____

3. _____   6. _____   9. _____   12. _____

Sentences Using Words with the **tion** Ending

Additional words with the **tion** ending:

dic**tion**	atten**tion**	convec**tion**	subtrac**tion**	interna**tion**al
frac**tion**	induc**tion**	inspec**tion**	conven**tion**al	ques**tion***
fric**tion**	inven**tion**	descrip**tion**	inten**tion**al	

*This word is pronounced "questyun."

Read:

1. Her description of the suction invention has conviction.
2. The international convention will be a big attraction.
3. Will you mention your intention to question her?
4. Addition and subtraction of fractions is an exam section.
5. Under no condition will I take action on that matter!
6. No attention was given to her bad diction.

Write:

1. _____

   _____

2. _____

   _____

3. _____

4. _____

   _____

5. _____

   _____

6. _____

   _____

Listen and write:

1. _____

2. _____

Special Skill

PREVIEWING WORDS OF THREE OR MORE SYLLABLES
FROM THE STORY The Crystal Junction Banner

Remember that each syllable has one vowel sound.

Read syllables:	Read words:	Write the words:
1. a bys mal	abysmal	*abysmal*
2. ad dic tion	addiction	
3. ad di tion	addition	
4. ad di tion al	additional	
5. ad dress ing	addressing	
6. ad vanc ing	advancing	
7. an a lyt i cal	analytical	
8. an oth er	another	
9. at ten tive	attentive	
10. at trac tion	attraction	
11. band wag on	bandwagon	
12. ben e fits	benefits	
13. cit i zens	citizens	
14. com bat ing	combating	
15. com bat ive	combative	
16. com mit ted	committed	
17. con di tions	conditions	
18. con gress man	congressman	
19. con sen sus	consensus	
20. con struc tion	construction	
21. con vec tion	convection	
22. con ven tion	convention	
23. con ven tion al	conventional	

Read syllables:	Read words:	Write the words:
24. con vic tions	convictions	_____
25. e co nom ic	economic	_____
26. e lec tive	elective	_____
27. ex cel lent	excellent	_____
28. ex ten sive ly	extensively	_____
29. fed er al	federal	_____
30. fed er al ly	federally	_____
31. fun da men tals	fundamentals	_____
32. gov ern ment	government	_____
33. gym nas tics	gymnastics	_____
34. hyp not ic	hypnotic	_____
35. hys ter i cal	hysterical	_____
36. im per a tive	imperative	_____
37. im ple ment ing	implementing	_____
38. im pres sive	impressive	_____
39. in cen tive	incentive	_____
40. in cum bent	incumbent	_____
41. in duc tion	induction	_____
42. in dus try	industry	_____
43. in quis i tive	inquisitive	_____
44. in sen si tive	insensitive	_____
45. in spec tion	inspection	_____
46. in struc tion	instruction	_____
47. in ten tion	intention	_____
48. in ter na tion al	international	_____
49. in ven tions	inventions	_____
50. min er al	mineral	_____

Read syllables:	Read words:	Write the words:
51. mud sling ing	mudslinging	_____
52. na tion al	national	_____
53. ob jec tive	objective	_____
54. of fen sive	offensive	_____
55. per spec tive	perspective	_____
56. po lit i cal	political	_____
57. po si tion	position	_____
58. pos i tive	positive	_____
59. pres i dent	president	_____
60. pro duc tion	production	_____
61. rel a tives	relatives	_____
62. se lec tive	selective	_____
63. sen si tive	sensitive	_____
64. sub jec tive	subjective	_____
65. sub trac tion	subtraction	_____
66. syl la bles	syllables	_____
67. sym pa thy	sympathy	_____
68. syn op sis	synopsis	_____
69. syn thet ic	synthetic	_____
70. sys tem at ic	systematic	_____
71. typ i cal	typical	_____
72. tyr an ny	tyranny	_____
73. un con ven tion al	unconventional	_____
74. un der stand	understand	_____

Listen and write:

1. _____
2. _____
3. _____
4. _____
5. _____
6. _____
7. _____
8. _____
9. _____
10. _____
11. _____
12. _____
13. _____
14. _____
15. _____
16. _____
17. _____
18. _____
19. _____
20. _____
21. _____
22. _____
23. _____
24. _____
25. _____
26. _____
27. _____
28. _____
29. _____
31. _____
30. _____
32. _____
33. _____
34. _____
35. _____
36. _____
37. _____
38. _____
39. _____
40. _____
41. _____
42. _____
43. _____
44. _____
45. _____
46. _____
47. _____
48. _____
49. _____
50. _____
51. _____
52. _____
53. _____
54. _____
55. _____
56. _____

Story 12

THE CRYSTAL JUNCTION BANNER
WEDNESDAY, JULY 26, 1989

Member of Congress Flynn Running for Top Elective Office

Lynn Plympton
Banner Staff

CRYSTAL JUNCTION—At the political convention held today at the Civic Center, Congressman Lyndon Flynn said he is running for President. Flynn asked citizens to jump on his bandwagon to put him in this top elective office. Flynn said, "When I'm President, today will be better than yesterday."

Flynn addressed the citizens on his political positions:

—Bringing jobs in the construction industry to Crystal Junction. "This economic incentive will be an attraction to live in the city."

—Backing the synthetic metals project and gypsum mineral production.

—Advancing adoption of inventions in industry, such as convection current.

—Getting rid of graft in federally funded projects. "Graft is a typical symptom of problems in the federal government today. A lot of friction exists in Congress on this subject."

> **"When I'm President, today will be better than yesterday."**
> **—Lyndon Flynn**

—Bringing justice back to the induction methods of the Selective Service (the draft).

—Implementing extensive unconventional tax benefits.

FLYNN FOR PRESIDENT, Page 4

FLYNN FOR PRESIDENT
Continued from Page 1

Flynn said, "The incumbent is insensitive to the citizens' problems with the income-tax system!"

—Backing better instruction for children in the fundamentals of addition, subtraction, and fractions so they can advance. "It's imperative to have additional classes for inquisitive children and for gymnastics, too."

—Addressing the problems of drug addiction. "I will get fast convictions of the pushers!"

"I have traveled extensively, and am an expert in international politics. I was involved in the inspection of missiles with the Kremlin."

Flynn added, "I'm committed to combating tyranny when I'm President!"

Citizens question Flynn

Citizens were attentive to what Flynn said. Some were pensive and passive; others were combative and offensive. His critics said, "Flynn's mudslinging tactics have to go, or we aren't backing him on the ballot!"

A synopsis of the citizens' comments on Flynn's political positions was:

—Some said he had an analytical method with problems that was impressive.

—Others said he was sensitive and systematic.

—A person added that Flynn was subjective, not objective, since he had relatives in the construction industry and in the federal government.

—From another perspective, some said he had sympathy for the abysmal conditions in the slums.

—Some said they were glad Flynn mentioned his intention to exert positive action on drug addiction.

—Others added that Flynn's diction was excellent. "We can understand his syllables."

—Another person added, "But I can't understand his syntax."

"Flynn's mudslinging tactics have to go, or we aren't backing him on the ballot!"
                                        —Flynn's critics

—Gladys Dylan said, "I wasn't backing Flynn yesterday. My husband and brother weren't backing him, but since this convention, we will back him. It's impressive to have him tell us his political position in person. That's very helpful! I haven't met a member of Congress as strong as he is. Flynn isn't bad. I'm positive we aren't going to get a better President. He hasn't misled us!"

Man of strong convictions

The consensus was that "Flynn's got strong convictions." Flynn addressed the citizens in a conventional manner. He was not hypnotic or hysterical, but he said what he wanted.

At the end of the convention, Flynn led the citizens in singing the national anthem.

Story 12 emphasizes:
- contractions: **it's, that's, he's, she's, I'm, isn't, aren't, wasn't, weren't, hasn't, haven't, can't, *noun*'s**
- **y = ĭ; ive, tion**

and includes selections from:
- two-syllable, short-vowel words and names
- verb + **s** (third-person singular); noun + **'s** (possessive)
- special sounds: **ck, sh, ch, tch, th, wh, ce, ci, ge, gi, dge**
- initial and final blends
- other endings: **le, al, y, ly, ing, ang, ong, ung, eng, ink, ank, onk, unk, enk, ed, er**
- sight words: **for, or, want, too, women, today, yesterday, was, were, nothing, what, from**
- three or more syllable, short-vowel words (see list on page 222–224)

Appendices

Appendix A: Sight Words

I. REVIEW OF BOOK ONE SIGHT WORDS

have	me	live	a		**to be**			**Colors**	
	he	give	the	I am		we are		red	black
said	she		come	you are		you are		yellow	white
	we	I	some	(singular)		(plural)		blue	brown
they	be		son	he is		they are		orange	tan
		are		she is				green	gray
full	do		no	it is				purple	pink
pull	to	her	go						
put	you		so						

Numbers

0	zero	10	ten	20	twenty
1	one	11	eleven	21	twenty-one
2	two	12	twelve	22	twenty-two
3	three	13	thirteen	23	twenty-three
4	four	14	fourteen	24	twenty-four
5	five	15	fifteen	25	twenty-five
6	six	16	sixteen	26	twenty-six
7	seven	17	seventeen	27	twenty-seven
8	eight	18	eighteen	28	twenty-eight
9	nine	19	nineteen	29	twenty-nine

30	thirty	40	forty	50	fifty
31	thirty-one	41	forty-one	51	fifty-one
39	thirty-nine	49	forty-nine	59	fifty-nine

60	sixty	70	seventy	80	eighty
61	sixty-one	71	seventy-one	81	eighty-one
69	sixty-nine	79	seventy-nine	89	eighty-nine

90	ninety	100	one hundred	100,000	one hundred thousand
91	ninety-one	1,000	one thousand	1,000,000	one million
99	ninety-nine	10,000	ten thousand	1,000,000,000	one billion

The Calendar

12 Months of the Year

January	July
February	August
March	September
April	October
May	November
June	December

7 Days of the Week

Sunday

Monday

Tuesday

Wednesday

Thursday

Friday

Saturday

The Clock

 It's one o'clock.

 It's a quarter past two (two-fifteen).

 It's half-past three (three-thirty).

 It's a quarter to five (four forty-five).

 It's five minutes past five (five past five; five after five).

 It's twenty minutes to seven (twenty to seven; six-forty).

II. NEW SIGHT WORDS FROM BOOK TWO

Short Vowels Instead of the Schwa (ə)

In this series, for the purposes of learning to read, the sound of a vowel is considered short if it is not long. Thus, the sounds frequently represented in dictionaries as ə are taught here as short vowels. For example:

Word	Webster's Ninth New Collegiate™ Dictionary*	Essentials of Reading and Writing English
selective	sə lek tiv	sĕ lĕc tĭve
political	pə lit i cal	pŏ lĭt ĭ căl
summit	səm ət	sŭm mĭt

Exceptions, as previously noted, are **o** = **ŭ** (s**o**n = s**u**n) and **u** as in **pull**.

---

*Copyright ©1986 by Merriam-Webster Inc.

Page	Word
7	women
13	for
13	or
13	want
13	too
23	today
23	yesterday
26	was
26	were
53	they
55	thing
55	nothing
55	think
55	thank
56	something
57	what
149	England
194	father
221	question

Words and Names in Which *o* Sounds Like *ŭ* (son = sun)

Page 11

ransom	lemon	felon	Paxton
bottom	gallon	ribbon	Milton
custom	wagon	London	Wilson
wisdom	melon	cotton	Benson
seldom	lesson	button	Nelson
	canyon	Boston	

Page	Word
41	haddock
56	month
60	solicit
79	from
105	front
136	nothing
136	something

Page	Word
136	Lexington
194	mother
194	brother
194	grandmother
198	another
198	customers

Words and Names with *ŭ* (as in pull)

Page	Word	Page	Word
43	bush	7	bull
43	push	7	bullet
173	bushed	18	bulletin
173	pushed	47	Butch

Appendix B:
Alphabetical List of Introductory Two-Syllable, Short-Vowel Words and Names

These words are presented in the text on pages 4–12.

A
Adam
admit
ago
Allen
amid
amiss
Anna
annex
antic
Anton
attic

B
bandit
basket
Benson
Boston
bottom
boxes
bullet*
button
buzzes

C
cabin
cactus
caftan
Calvin
camel

campus
candid
cannot
canvas
canyon
carrot
catnap
catnip
coffin
Collin
combat
comet
comic
commit
compass
compel
confess
cotton
custom
cutlet

D
denim
Dennis
discuss
dismiss
dispel
Donna

E
Edwin
Ellen

embed
exam
exit
expel

F
fatten
felon
fitful
fitness
fulfill

G
gallon
gavel
gotten

H
habit
Hanna
happen
hatless
hectic
Helen
helmet
hidden
hubcap

I
illness
impel
index

inlet
input
inset
into

J
Janet
jobless

K
Kansas
Karen
Kevin
kidnap
kitten

L
lemon
lentils
lessen
lesson
limit
Linda
linen
liquid
London

M
magnet
mallet
Maxwell
Megan

melon
Melvin
messes
Milton
misfit
mishap
misled
mitten
mixes
muffin
muslin

N
napkin
Nelson
nutmeg

O
offset
onset
optic

P
pallid
panel
panic
passes
Paxton
pelvis
picnic
public
puppet

Q
quintet

R
rabbit
ramrod
ransom
rapid
ribbon
rimless
Robin
rotten
rustic

S
sadness
salad
satin
seldom
seven
solid
sublet
submit
sudden
sunset
sunup

T
tablet
tactic

talent
tennis
tidbit
tonic
tonsils

U
uncut
unfit
unless
until
uphill
upon
upset

V
valid
victim
visit
vomit

W
wagon
welcome*
willful
Wilson
wisdom
witness
women*

X–Y–Z
zigzag

*sight word

Appendix C:
Geography—Some Places with Short-Vowel Names

I. WORLD

A. Countries
the Bahamas
Bangladesh
Benin
Botswana
Brazil
Canada
Central African
    Republic
Chad
Finland
France
Gabon
Germany
Italy
Japan
Kenya
Lebanon
the Netherlands
Pakistan
Panama
Vatican City
Yemen
Zimbabwe

B. Oceans
Atlantic
Pacific

C. Great Rivers
Amazon
Angara
Back
Bug
Don
Drava
Indus
Nelson
Parana
Red
Shannon
Yellow

D. Other Places
Athens
Bangkok
Calcutta
Caracas
Dublin
Havana
Hong Kong
Istanbul
Leningrad
Lisbon
London
Madrid
Manila
Milan
Scotland
Tibet
Tonkin Gulf

II. UNITED STATES (USA)

A. States
Alabama
Alaska
Florida
Kansas
Kentucky
Montana
Nebraska
Nevada
Texas
Vermont
Wisconsin

B. Capital Cities*
Atlanta (GA)
Boston (MA)
Columbus (OH)
Denver (CO)
Helena (MT)
Jackson (MS)
Jefferson City (MO)
Little Rock (AR)
Madison (WI)
Providence (RI)
Richmond (VA)
Trenton (NJ)

C. Other Cities
Amherst
Bethesda
Beverly Hills
Breckenridge
Brockton
Bronx (the)
Bunker Hill
Camden
Chester
Dallas
Essex
Evanston
Grafton
Hackensack
Livingston
Lynn
Lubbock
Paramus
Paterson
Silver Spring
Stockbridge
Tampa
Westchester
Westland
West Mifflin
Yonkers

*Post Office-authorized two-letter state abbreviations follow each capital city.

Appendix D:
Idioms

I. IDIOMS IN BOOK TWO

These idioms use the sounds and words you have learned.

Chapter	Page	Idiom	Definition
1	17	to come up with	to provide for; to produce results
1	17	to go for it	to try to get; to do with enthusiasm
2	37	to be let go	to be fired, laid off from a job
2	37	to tell off	to speak bluntly or rudely to
2	37	to have had it	not to tolerate any more
2	37	to get on with it	to do something without delay
3	50	to be sick of it	to be tired of or disgusted with something
3	51	a lot of bucks	a lot of money
3	52	to itch for	to have a desire for; to want strongly
3	52	to pack it in	to eat a lot of food quickly
3	69	to be on the bench	(1) legal: to judge; to be seated, to preside in court (2) athletics: to be removed from or kept out of a game
3	70	to get with it	to be aware; to do what is necessary
3	70	to be a cutup	to act in a comic or unruly manner
3	70	to let you off	to release; to permit to go (with little or no penalty)
3	70	to be in with	to be part of a certain group
4	91	to grill	to question intensively
4	91	to put on the track	to direct a person or action
4	91	to be stuck in a rut	to do something over and over again
4	103	to the hilt	as much as possible
4	103	kept it up	continued; persisted
4	110	to have a lot of jazz	to be exciting, dazzling
4	112	it's a trick not to	it's difficult not to
4	112	do not bug	do not bother or annoy
4	112	to crash	(1) to collapse with fatigue (2) to attend an event without an invitation
5	165	a hang-up	a problem
5	165	to ring you up	to telephone you
5	166	punching the clock	on the job: using a time card to record the hours worked; time in and time out of work

Chapter	Page	Idiom	Definition
5	184	to be sacked	to be fired, dismissed from a job
5	186	to be bushed	to be exhausted, worn out
6	205	to be onto someone	not to be fooled by a person or action; to be aware
6	205	to be on a fast track	to want to attain one's goal quickly, sometimes disregarding others
6	205	to get one's number	not to be fooled by a person; to be aware of what someone's actions mean
6	226	to jump on the bandwagon	to join a cause; to participate in an activity, sometimes political

II. ADDITIONAL IDIOMS

You can read these idioms using the phonetic sounds learned in Book Two.

Idiom	Definition	Phonetic Element and Chapter
1. to button one's lip	to stop speaking	two-syllable, short-vowel word, 1

—He buttoned his lip when she ran in since he was discussing her.

| 2. to be on the level | to be honest | two-syllable, short-vowel word, 1 |

—She is on the level; you can do what she recommends.

| 3. to go bananas | to act excited, crazy, wild | three-syllable, short-vowel word, 1 |

—The kids went bananas when they won the contest.

| 4. to be in for it | to get into trouble | sight word **for**, 1 |

—The felon will be in for it when the judge passes sentence.

| 5. to get off his/her back | to stop bothering, nagging | **ck**, 3 |

—He told the boss to get off his back; he's doing the best he can.

| 6. to pass the buck | to shift responsibility or blame | **ck**, 3 |

—Jim will not do it; he'll pass the buck to Karen. Karen will not do it; she'll pass the buck to her assistant.

| 7. to kick up a fuss | to make trouble | **ck**, 3 |

—If we do not let them sing, will they kick up a fuss?

Idiom	Definition	Phonetic Element and Chapter
8. to catch on	to understand	**tch**, 3

—She can do the job; she catches on quickly.

| 9. to be fed up with | to be tired of or disgusted with | **th**, 3 |

—They are fed up with the task; it's dull.

| 10. to kick the bucket | to die | **ck**, 3 |

—He's not living; he kicked the bucket long ago.

| 11. to put in a plug for | to recommend | sight word **for**; **pl**, 1, 4 |

—The doctors on TV put in a plug for being fit.

| 12. to clam up | to stop talking; be silent | **cl**, 4 |

—He clammed up and said nothing when they yelled at him.

| 13. to be stuck on | (1) to be in love with | **ck, st**, 3, 4 |
| | (2) to be baffled by something | |

—(1) Robert is stuck on Beverly; he wants to marry her.
—(2) We are stuck on that problem; we cannot do it.

| 14. to put across | to explain successfully | **cr**, 4 |

—She put across the concept very well; they did understand.

| 15. to put the skids on | to stop suddenly | **sk**, 4 |

—When he lost his cash, he put the skids on his travel plans.

| 16. to do the trick | to solve the problem | **ck, tr**, 3, 4 |

—Letting him run will do the trick; then he will be happy.

| 17. to smell a rat | to be suspicious | **sm**, 4 |

—We think they are telling us fibs. We smell a rat!

| 18. to snap it up | (1) to go faster; hurry | **sn**, 4 |
| | (2) to grab something | |

—(1) If we snap it up, we can finish the job today.
—(2) It costs so little, we will snap it up.

| 19. to step on it | to go faster | **st**, 4 |

—I got into the cab and said, "Step on it! I'm in a hurry!"

| 20. to split | to leave | **spl**, 4 |

—She split from the ranch yesterday and did not come back.

| 21. to be fit as a fiddle | to be healthy, in good shape | **le**, 5 |

—I golf and jog and am fit as a fiddle.

| 22. to be in a pickle | to be in trouble | **ck, le**, 3, 5 |

—Since he did not finish the exam, he is in a pickle.

Idiom	Definition	Phonetic Element and Chapter
23. to be fishy	to be suspicious, not right	**sh, y**, 3, 5

—The offer for the split-level is fishy; we will not accept it.

| 24. to get the hang of | to understand how to do | **ang**, 5 |

—I understand; I get the hang of things quickly.

| 25. to wing it | to figure it out as you do it | **ing**, 5 |

—We do not have a map. We will have to wing it as we travel.

| 26. to swing it | to accomplish it | **sw, ing**, 4, 5 |

—Benjamin will do it. He can swing it.

| 27. to stop bugging someone | to stop bothering someone | **st, ing**, 4, 5 |

—Stop bugging him. He's doing the best he can.

| 28. to get stung | to be cheated or tricked | **st, ung**, 4, 5 |

—We are mad! We got stung with a bad check at the shop.

| 29. to pull strings | to use influence to get something | **str, ing**, 4,5 |

—Can you pull strings to get him a summer job?

| 30. to spring for | to pay for, to treat | *for,* **spr, ing**, 1, 4, 5 |

—Do not bother to bring cash. I will spring for lunch today.

| 31. to be off one's rocker | to be or act crazy | **ck, er**, 3, 5 |

—That comic must be off his rocker! He acts too silly.

| 32. to pocket the difference | to keep the change (money) | **ck, ce, er**, 3, 5 |

—After he sells the stock, he will pocket the difference.

| 33. can't hack it | (1) not to be able to do it
(2) not to be able to take the stress | **ck,** *can't,* 3, 6 |

—He will quit that job; he can't hack it.

| 34. can't stand it | not to be able to tolerate it | **st, nd,** *can't,* 4, 6 |

—She can't stand that job on the bus. She will quit.

| 35. to be chicken | to be scared to do something | **ch, ck**, 3 |

—They will not swim across the pond. They are chicken!

Appendix E: Common Last Names with Short Vowels, y Endings, and Color Sight Words

This is a list of some common last names with sounds that follow English phonetic rules. For example:

—**Chen** is included because the **Ch** and **en** are standard English sounds for those letters.

—**Juan** is not included because in this name **J = H**, which is not a standard English sound for that letter.

A
Abbott
Adams
Adler
Allen*
Anderson
Appleton

B
Bannister
Baxter
Becker
Bell
Bennett
Berger
Black**
Blackman
Brennan
Brown**
Butler

C
Callahan
Cassidy
Chan
Chang
Chen

Cheng
Chin
Chung
Collins
Cox

D
Dickinson
Donovan
Duffy
Duggan

E
Ellis
Emerson
Evans

F
Fisher
Flanagan
Flynn
Foster
Fox

G
Gibbons
Gibson
Gillis
Grant

Gray**
Green**
Griffin

H
Hamilton
Hansen
Hanson
Harrington
Harris
Higgins
Hill
Hoffman

J
Jackson
Jenkins
Jensen

K
Kelly
Kennedy
King

L
Levin
Lynch

M
Manning
MacMillan

Maxwell
McGrath
Miller
Mitchell*
Morris*

N
Nash
Nelson*
Nickerson

O
Ogden

P
Pappas
Perry*
Pratt

Q
Quinn

R
Roberts
Robinson
Ross*
Russell*

S
Sanders
Scott*

Simmons
Singer
Smith
Sullivan

T
Talbot
Tran
Tucker

U
Unger

V
Vance
Vincent*

W
Wang
Webster
West
White**
Wilkinson
Wilson
Wong

X-Y-Z
Yung
Zimmerman

---

*These are common first names, too.
**These are color sight words.

Appendix F:
Summary of Sounds and Words in the Stories in Book Two

I. PHONETIC ELEMENTS AND SIGHT WORDS

Each story emphasizes the phonetic elements and sight words taught in its chapter and includes and reviews those from previous stories and chapters. To determine the contents of a story, read upwards on the chart.

Chapter (Page) Title	Phonetic Elements Emphasized:	Sight Words
1 (16) The Picnic at Cactus Canyon	two-syllable, short-vowel words and names [0*]	for, or, want, too, women
2 (37) Helen's Lesson	Verb + s (third-person singular) Noun + 's (possessive) [0*]	today, yesterday, was, were
3 (51) Chen's Chuck Wagon	**ck, sh, ch, tch** [0*]	—
3 (69) Justice Comes to Ridgeton	**th, wh, ce, ci, ge, gi, dge** [11*]	thing, something, nothing, think, thank, what
4 (89) The Drop-In Clinic	initial blends with **l, r, s, c, k, m, n, p, t, w** [6*]	from
4 (102) Camp West Wind	final blends with **ct, ft, ld, lf, lk, lm, lp, lt, mp, nd, nt, pt, sk, sp, st** [6*]	—
4 (110) Trent's Dress and Pants Shop	initial and final blends [8*]	—
5 (133) The Dance Academy's Festival	endings: **le, al, y, ly** [27*]	—
5 (164) The Franklin Fish Packing Plant	**ing, ang, ong, ung, eng, ink, ank, onk, unk, enk** [4*]	—

*The number of words and names of three or more syllables using these phonetic elements; see Part II for this list.

I. PHONETIC ELEMENTS AND SIGHT WORDS (Cont'd.)

5 (183) We Visited Uncle Ned's Cattle Ranch — **ed** past tense (sounds like **id, d, t**) and **ed** general [24*]

5 (202) Mr. Webster's Day at the Bunker Hill Bank — **er** [77*]

6 (226) The Crystal Junction Banner — contractions: **it's, that's, he's, she's, I'm, isn't, aren't, wasn't, weren't, hasn't, haven't, can't, noun's; y = ĭ**; ive, tion [74*]

II. THREE OR MORE SYLLABLE WORDS AND NAMES

Chapter (Page) Title	List of Three or More Syllable Words and Names:
1 (16) The **Picnic** at **Cactus** Canyon	[none]
2 (37) Helen's Lesson	[none]
3 (51) **Chen's Chuck** Wagon	[none]
3 (69) Justice Comes to Ridgeton	[11] **agenda**, alleges, benefit, cabinet, **citizens**, illicit, maximum, minimum, sentences, **solicit**, witnesses
4 (89) The Drop-In Clinic	[6] benefit, **blemishes**, cinnamon, epidemic, gelatin, regimen
4 (102) **Camp West Wind**	[6] catamaran, **contestant**, eleven, epilog, habitat, javelin
4 (110) **Trent's Dress** and Pants Shop	[8] bandannas, catalog, elegant, **excellent**, moccasins, taffeta; Panama, **Priscilla**
5 (133) The Dance Academy's Festival	[27] academy, **blueberry, bottlebrush, bottleneck**, classical, comical, competent, confident, cranberry, excellent, festival, gelatins, hospitality, marimba, metallic, pedestal, pivotal, principal, prominent, sentimental, splendidly, tactfully, timidly; **Cassidy**, Donnelson, Kennedy, Mexican
5 (164) The **Franklin Fish** Packing Plant	[4] benefi**ting**, family, finishes, finishing

*The number of words and names of three or more syllables using these phonetic elements; see Part II for this list.

5 (183) We Visited Uncle Ned's Cattle Ranch

[24] accomplished, adapted, admitted, animals, astonished, budgeted, bulleted, collected, difficult, difficulty, embedded, exited, expected, fantastic, fidgeted, hospitality, invested, jackrabbits, possible, spirited, talented, unexpectedly, upcoming, visited

5 (202) Mr. Webster's Day at the Bunker Hill Bank

[77] administers, aftermath, agenda, another, assisted, blithering, blockbuster, bobsledders, caliber, citizens, collateral, considered, customers, discusses, elderly, encumber, establishment, existence, expected, external, family, federal, fingertips, fluttering, forever, fraternal, government, grandfather, grandmother, hankering, happily, helicopter, inherited*, intercontinental, interest**, internal, interpreted, interrupted, intervals, investment, lavender, liberal, limited, manager, officer, passenger, personal, personnel, properly, property, registered, residents, sentinel, several**, suspected, suspenders, terrific, together, travelers, understanding, veteran, visited, windjammer, wonderful; Alberta, American, Anderson, Atlantic, Beverly, Emerson, Henderson, Jennifer, Nantucket, Rochester, Switzerland, Vanderhoff, Winchester

6 (226) The Crystal Junction Banner

[74] abysmal, addiction, addition, additional, addressing, advancing, analytical, another, attentive, attraction, bandwagon, benefits, citizens, combating, combative, committed, conditions, congressman, consensus, construction, convection, convention, conventional, convictions, economic, elective, excellent, extensively, federal, federally, fundamentals, government, gymnastics, hypnotic, hysterical, imperative, implementing, impressive, incentive, incumbent, induction, industry, inquisitive, insensitive, inspection, instruction, intention, international, inventions, mineral, mudslinging, national, objective, offensive, perspective, political, position, positive, president, production, relatives, selective, sensitive, subjective, subtraction, syllables, sympathy, synopsis, synthetic, systematic, typical, tyranny, unconventional, understand

*short ĕ (ĕgg) sound, not er
**usually pronounced in two syllables

About the Authors

Judith S. Rubenstein received a Doctorate in Education from Harvard University and a B.A. in French from Wellesley College. Dr. Rubenstein has taught English language skills abroad and in Massachusetts (Harvard University Extension School, adult education programs, and private practice). She has published articles on various subjects in *The Boston Globe, The Journal of the American Medical Association, Adolescence,* and *Nature,* as well as having written, edited, and translated English and foreign language materials. As an educational consultant, Dr. Rubenstein is committed to teaching adults and children how to communicate effectively on many levels. Currently, she is creating a wide range of learning materials for speakers of English and other languages.

Janet M. Gubbay received a B.S. in sociology and anthropology from Northeastern University and studied counseling at the Northeastern Graduate School of Education. She is an experienced project leader, researcher, writer, editor, and book designer. As a writer and editor, she is committed to creating learning materials that promote personal growth and enrichment for people of all ages and backgrounds. Currently, she is writing books for children that focus on building self-esteem and encouraging independence of thought.